C-3646 CAREER EXAMINATION SERIES

This is your
PASSBOOK for...

Qualifying Resources Recovery Operator (QRO)

Test Preparation Study Guide
Questions & Answers

NATIONAL LEARNING CORPORATION®

COPYRIGHT NOTICE

This book is SOLELY intended for, is sold ONLY to, and its use is RESTRICTED to individual, bona fide applicants or candidates who qualify by virtue of having seriously filed applications for appropriate license, certificate, professional and/or promotional advancement, higher school matriculation, scholarship, or other legitimate requirements of education and/or governmental authorities.

This book is NOT intended for use, class instruction, tutoring, training, duplication, copying, reprinting, excerption, or adaptation, etc., by:

1) Other publishers
2) Proprietors and/or Instructors of "Coaching" and/or Preparatory Courses
3) Personnel and/or Training Divisions of commercial, industrial, and governmental organizations
4) Schools, colleges, or universities and/or their departments and staffs, including teachers and other personnel
5) Testing Agencies or Bureaus
6) Study groups which seek by the purchase of a single volume to copy and/or duplicate and/or adapt this material for use by the group as a whole without having purchased individual volumes for each of the members of the group
7) Et al.

Such persons would be in violation of appropriate Federal and State statutes.

PROVISION OF LICENSING AGREEMENTS – Recognized educational, commercial, industrial, and governmental institutions and organizations, and others legitimately engaged in educational pursuits, including training, testing, and measurement activities, may address request for a licensing agreement to the copyright owners, who will determine whether, and under what conditions, including fees and charges, the materials in this book may be used them. In other words, a licensing facility exists for the legitimate use of the material in this book on other than an individual basis. However, it is asseverated and affirmed here that the material in this book CANNOT be used without the receipt of the express permission of such a licensing agreement from the Publishers. Inquiries re licensing should be addressed to the company, attention rights and permissions department.

All rights reserved, including the right of reproduction in whole or in part, in any form or by any means, electronic or mechanical, including photocopying, recording, or by any information storage and retrieval system, without permission in writing from the Publisher.

Copyright © 2024 by
National Learning Corporation

212 Michael Drive, Syosset, NY 11791
(516) 921-8888 • www.passbooks.com
E-mail: info@passbooks.com

PASSBOOK® SERIES

THE *PASSBOOK® SERIES* has been created to prepare applicants and candidates for the ultimate academic battlefield – the examination room.

At some time in our lives, each and every one of us may be required to take an examination – for validation, matriculation, admission, qualification, registration, certification, or licensure.

Based on the assumption that every applicant or candidate has met the basic formal educational standards, has taken the required number of courses, and read the necessary texts, the *PASSBOOK® SERIES* furnishes the one special preparation which may assure passing with confidence, instead of failing with insecurity. Examination questions – together with answers – are furnished as the basic vehicle for study so that the mysteries of the examination and its compounding difficulties may be eliminated or diminished by a sure method.

This book is meant to help you pass your examination provided that you qualify and are serious in your objective.

The entire field is reviewed through the huge store of content information which is succinctly presented through a provocative and challenging approach – the question-and-answer method.

A climate of success is established by furnishing the correct answers at the end of each test.

You soon learn to recognize types of questions, forms of questions, and patterns of questioning. You may even begin to anticipate expected outcomes.

You perceive that many questions are repeated or adapted so that you can gain acute insights, which may enable you to score many sure points.

You learn how to confront new questions, or types of questions, and to attack them confidently and work out the correct answers.

You note objectives and emphases, and recognize pitfalls and dangers, so that you may make positive educational adjustments.

Moreover, you are kept fully informed in relation to new concepts, methods, practices, and directions in the field.

You discover that you are actually taking the examination all the time: you are preparing for the examination by "taking" an examination, not by reading extraneous and/or supererogatory textbooks.

In short, this PASSBOOK®, used directedly, should be an important factor in helping you to pass your test.

QRO

SCOPE OF THE QUALIFYING RESOURCES RECOVERY OPERATED (QRO) CERTIFICATION PROGRAM

The QRO Certification Program is intended for persons who hold, or wish to hold, the following positions at a resource recovery facility:

Chief Facility Operator: The chief facility operator is the person in direct charge and control of the operation of a resource recovery facility and is responsible for overall on-site supervision, technical direction, management, and performance of the facility including, but not limited to:

1. overall operation, maintenance, and performance of the facility;
2. operation in accordance with established facility policies and, procedures;
3. assuring facility personnel are qualified and certified as required and trained when applicable federal, state and local environmental regulations, or plant technology, plant policies, or plant procedures are changed;
4. assuring facility operation is consistent with applicable federal, state, and local environmental requirements;
5. communication with regulatory agencies;
6. assuring policies and procedures, for proper and safe plant operations are formulated and updated periodically.

Shift Supervisor: The shift supervisor is the person in direct charge and control of the operation of a resource recovery facility during an assigned shift including, but not limited to:

1. supervising, training, and monitoring performance of personnel during an assigned shift;
2. maintaining records of facility operations, including operational changes and abnormalities, and reports to chief facility operator;
3. authorizing issuance of work orders for equipment repair and maintenance;
4. assuring the facility is operated consistent with applicable federal, state, and local environmental requirements;
5. monitoring operations in accordance with established facility policies and procedures;
6. undertaking actions to correct upsets or emergencies;
7. assuring a safe workplace;
8. communicating operational status of plant with the relieving shift supervisor at shift turnover.

ELIGIBILITY REQUIREMENTS

Applicants must meet the following qualifications before taking the General Examination:

1. High school diploma or equivalent
2. Five years of experience in general industry, industrial process, or power plant operations. Completion of a baccalaureate degree in physical science or engineering, or 60 credits of cours work in the following subjects, from an institute accredited to issue baccalaureate degrees, may be substituted for up to two years of experience:
   a. advanced mathematics;
   b. chemistry;
   c. fluid dynamics;
   d. thermodynamics;
   e. materials science;
   f. combustion theory;
   g. environmental, mechanical, civil, chemical or electrical engineering.

EXAMINATION CONTENT

The examination will test understanding of the following topics:

1. interactions among the major facility systems;
2. principles of combustion;
3. safe procedures and practices;
4. operation of deaerator systems, cooling water chemistry, and feed water systems;
5. laboratory procedures, such as testing water samples;
6. boiler designs;
7. solid waste and residue landfilling;
8. the importance of planned and preventive maintenance programs required to maintain facility electrical, mechanical, and instrument equipment in optimum, reliable operating conditions;
9. weight scale equipment operation;
10. characteristics which make certain types of waste unprocessible in the facility;
11. waste condition which has a deleterious impact on handling, processing, feeding, or combustion
12. waste handling, processing, and feeding equipment design and operation;
13. operation of boilers and auxiliaries;
14. operation of ash handling equipment;
15. design and operation of facility waste water treatment equipment;
16. implementation and maintenance of electrical, mechanical, and instrumentation maintenance logging;
17. the start-up, shutdown, and operation modes of a turbine generator and its auxiliaries, including condenser and cooling tower systems;
18. the operation of steam, hot water, and/or chiller systems including load control, and communications with users.

Examination Subject Areas

Part I (25% of examination) - Solid waste collection, transfer, and management, covering the following:

- Municipal solid waste composition
- Collection techniques
- Seasonal and industrial impact on the character of refuse
- Ash disposal
- Landfills
- Composting
- Environmental public relations
- Environmental regulation and requirements

PART II (25% of examination) - Theory, covering following

• Combustion • Chemistry • Thermodynamics	• Material science • Mechanical and electrical operation and technology	• Air pollution control technology • Air emission stack monitoring

PART III (50% of examination) - Operation of a resource recovery facility, covering the following:

- Material handling equipment
- Boiler operations
- Generator and turbine operations
- Ash handling and disposal operations
- General operations and maintenance procedures and techniques
- Worker safety
- Control room operations
- Continuous emissions monitors and their calibration

The examination is a multiple choice, written examination made up of between 100 to 150 questions divided as shown in the above table.

CONDUCT OF EXAMINATION

Applicants will have six hours to complete the examination. It is a closed book examination, however, a non-programmable calculator is permitted.

NOTIFICATION OF RESULTS

In order to receive certification, applicants must correctly answer at least 50% of the questions in each part, and correctly answer 70% of the questions overall. Applicants will be notified of the results of the examination, including the percentage of correct answers within each part, within 30 days.

In the event that an applicant does not pass the examination, it may be retaken as frequently as it is offered.

For further information regarding examinations, contact:
QRO Certification
ASME - 8A
United Engineering Center
345 East 47th Street
New York, NY 10017-2392
(212) 605-3381
FAX (212) 605-8713

HOW TO TAKE A TEST

I. YOU MUST PASS AN EXAMINATION

A. WHAT EVERY CANDIDATE SHOULD KNOW

Examination applicants often ask us for help in preparing for the written test. What can I study in advance? What kinds of questions will be asked? How will the test be given? How will the papers be graded?

As an applicant for a civil service examination, you may be wondering about some of these things. Our purpose here is to suggest effective methods of advance study and to describe civil service examinations.

Your chances for success on this examination can be increased if you know how to prepare. Those "pre-examination jitters" can be reduced if you know what to expect. You can even experience an adventure in good citizenship if you know why civil service exams are given.

B. WHY ARE CIVIL SERVICE EXAMINATIONS GIVEN?

Civil service examinations are important to you in two ways. As a citizen, you want public jobs filled by employees who know how to do their work. As a job seeker, you want a fair chance to compete for that job on an equal footing with other candidates. The best-known means of accomplishing this two-fold goal is the competitive examination.

Exams are widely publicized throughout the nation. They may be administered for jobs in federal, state, city, municipal, town or village governments or agencies.

Any citizen may apply, with some limitations, such as the age or residence of applicants. Your experience and education may be reviewed to see whether you meet the requirements for the particular examination. When these requirements exist, they are reasonable and applied consistently to all applicants. Thus, a competitive examination may cause you some uneasiness now, but it is your privilege and safeguard.

C. HOW ARE CIVIL SERVICE EXAMS DEVELOPED?

Examinations are carefully written by trained technicians who are specialists in the field known as "psychological measurement," in consultation with recognized authorities in the field of work that the test will cover. These experts recommend the subject matter areas or skills to be tested; only those knowledges or skills important to your success on the job are included. The most reliable books and source materials available are used as references. Together, the experts and technicians judge the difficulty level of the questions.

Test technicians know how to phrase questions so that the problem is clearly stated. Their ethics do not permit "trick" or "catch" questions. Questions may have been tried out on sample groups, or subjected to statistical analysis, to determine their usefulness.

Written tests are often used in combination with performance tests, ratings of training and experience, and oral interviews. All of these measures combine to form the best-known means of finding the right person for the right job.

II. HOW TO PASS THE WRITTEN TEST

A. NATURE OF THE EXAMINATION

To prepare intelligently for civil service examinations, you should know how they differ from school examinations you have taken. In school you were assigned certain definite pages to read or subjects to cover. The examination questions were quite detailed and usually emphasized memory. Civil service exams, on the other hand, try to discover your present ability to perform the duties of a position, plus your potentiality to learn these duties. In other words, a civil service exam attempts to predict how successful you will be. Questions cover such a broad area that they cannot be as minute and detailed as school exam questions.

In the public service similar kinds of work, or positions, are grouped together in one "class." This process is known as *position-classification*. All the positions in a class are paid according to the salary range for that class. One class title covers all of these positions, and they are all tested by the same examination.

B. FOUR BASIC STEPS

1) Study the announcement

How, then, can you know what subjects to study? Our best answer is: "Learn as much as possible about the class of positions for which you've applied." The exam will test the knowledge, skills and abilities needed to do the work.

Your most valuable source of information about the position you want is the official exam announcement. This announcement lists the training and experience qualifications. Check these standards and apply only if you come reasonably close to meeting them.

The brief description of the position in the examination announcement offers some clues to the subjects which will be tested. Think about the job itself. Review the duties in your mind. Can you perform them, or are there some in which you are rusty? Fill in the blank spots in your preparation.

Many jurisdictions preview the written test in the exam announcement by including a section called "Knowledge and Abilities Required," "Scope of the Examination," or some similar heading. Here you will find out specifically what fields will be tested.

2) Review your own background

Once you learn in general what the position is all about, and what you need to know to do the work, ask yourself which subjects you already know fairly well and which need improvement. You may wonder whether to concentrate on improving your strong areas or on building some background in your fields of weakness. When the announcement has specified "some knowledge" or "considerable knowledge," or has used adjectives like "beginning principles of..." or "advanced ... methods," you can get a clue as to the number and difficulty of questions to be asked in any given field. More questions, and hence broader coverage, would be included for those subjects which are more important in the work. Now weigh your strengths and weaknesses against the job requirements and prepare accordingly.

3) Determine the level of the position

Another way to tell how intensively you should prepare is to understand the level of the job for which you are applying. Is it the entering level? In other words, is this the position in which beginners in a field of work are hired? Or is it an intermediate or advanced level? Sometimes this is indicated by such words as "Junior" or "Senior" in the class title. Other jurisdictions use Roman numerals to designate the level – Clerk I, Clerk II, for example. The word "Supervisor" sometimes appears in the title. If the level is not indicated by the title, check the description of duties. Will you be working under very close supervision, or will you have responsibility for independent decisions in this work?

4) Choose appropriate study materials

Now that you know the subjects to be examined and the relative amount of each subject to be covered, you can choose suitable study materials. For beginning level jobs, or even advanced ones, if you have a pronounced weakness in some aspect of your training, read a modern, standard textbook in that field. Be sure it is up to date and has general coverage. Such books are normally available at your library, and the librarian will be glad to help you locate one. For entry-level positions, questions of appropriate difficulty are chosen – neither highly advanced questions, nor those too simple. Such questions require careful thought but not advanced training.

If the position for which you are applying is technical or advanced, you will read more advanced, specialized material. If you are already familiar with the basic principles of your field, elementary textbooks would waste your time. Concentrate on advanced textbooks and technical periodicals. Think through the concepts and review difficult problems in your field.

These are all general sources. You can get more ideas on your own initiative, following these leads. For example, training manuals and publications of the government agency which employs workers in your field can be useful, particularly for technical and professional positions. A letter or visit to the government department involved may result in more specific study suggestions, and certainly will provide you with a more definite idea of the exact nature of the position you are seeking.

III. KINDS OF TESTS

Tests are used for purposes other than measuring knowledge and ability to perform specified duties. For some positions, it is equally important to test ability to make adjustments to new situations or to profit from training. In others, basic mental abilities not dependent on information are essential. Questions which test these things may not appear as pertinent to the duties of the position as those which test for knowledge and information. Yet they are often highly important parts of a fair examination. For very general questions, it is almost impossible to help you direct your study efforts. What we can do is to point out some of the more common of these general abilities needed in public service positions and describe some typical questions.

1) General information

Broad, general information has been found useful for predicting job success in some kinds of work. This is tested in a variety of ways, from vocabulary lists to questions about current events. Basic background in some field of work, such as sociology or economics, may be sampled in a group of questions. Often these are principles which have become familiar to most persons through exposure rather than through formal training. It is difficult to advise you how to study for these questions; being alert to the world around you is our best suggestion.

2) Verbal ability

An example of an ability needed in many positions is verbal or language ability. Verbal ability is, in brief, the ability to use and understand words. Vocabulary and grammar tests are typical measures of this ability. Reading comprehension or paragraph interpretation questions are common in many kinds of civil service tests. You are given a paragraph of written material and asked to find its central meaning.

3) Numerical ability

Number skills can be tested by the familiar arithmetic problem, by checking paired lists of numbers to see which are alike and which are different, or by interpreting charts and graphs. In the latter test, a graph may be printed in the test booklet which you are asked to use as the basis for answering questions.

4) Observation

A popular test for law-enforcement positions is the observation test. A picture is shown to you for several minutes, then taken away. Questions about the picture test your ability to observe both details and larger elements.

5) Following directions

In many positions in the public service, the employee must be able to carry out written instructions dependably and accurately. You may be given a chart with several columns, each column listing a variety of information. The questions require you to carry out directions involving the information given in the chart.

6) Skills and aptitudes

Performance tests effectively measure some manual skills and aptitudes. When the skill is one in which you are trained, such as typing or shorthand, you can practice. These tests are often very much like those given in business school or high school courses. For many of the other skills and aptitudes, however, no short-time preparation can be made. Skills and abilities natural to you or that you have developed throughout your lifetime are being tested.

Many of the general questions just described provide all the data needed to answer the questions and ask you to use your reasoning ability to find the answers. Your best preparation for these tests, as well as for tests of facts and ideas, is to be at your physical and mental best. You, no doubt, have your own methods of getting into an exam-taking mood and keeping "in shape." The next section lists some ideas on this subject.

IV. KINDS OF QUESTIONS

Only rarely is the "essay" question, which you answer in narrative form, used in civil service tests. Civil service tests are usually of the short-answer type. Full instructions for answering these questions will be given to you at the examination. But in case this is your first experience with short-answer questions and separate answer sheets, here is what you need to know:

1) Multiple-choice Questions

Most popular of the short-answer questions is the "multiple choice" or "best answer" question. It can be used, for example, to test for factual knowledge, ability to solve problems or judgment in meeting situations found at work.

A multiple-choice question is normally one of three types—
- It can begin with an incomplete statement followed by several possible endings. You are to find the one ending which *best* completes the statement, although some of the others may not be entirely wrong.
- It can also be a complete statement in the form of a question which is answered by choosing one of the statements listed.

- It can be in the form of a problem – again you select the best answer.

Here is an example of a multiple-choice question with a discussion which should give you some clues as to the method for choosing the right answer:

When an employee has a complaint about his assignment, the action which will *best* help him overcome his difficulty is to
- A. discuss his difficulty with his coworkers
- B. take the problem to the head of the organization
- C. take the problem to the person who gave him the assignment
- D. say nothing to anyone about his complaint

In answering this question, you should study each of the choices to find which is best. Consider choice "A" – Certainly an employee may discuss his complaint with fellow employees, but no change or improvement can result, and the complaint remains unresolved. Choice "B" is a poor choice since the head of the organization probably does not know what assignment you have been given, and taking your problem to him is known as "going over the head" of the supervisor. The supervisor, or person who made the assignment, is the person who can clarify it or correct any injustice. Choice "C" is, therefore, correct. To say nothing, as in choice "D," is unwise. Supervisors have and interest in knowing the problems employees are facing, and the employee is seeking a solution to his problem.

2) True/False Questions

The "true/false" or "right/wrong" form of question is sometimes used. Here a complete statement is given. Your job is to decide whether the statement is right or wrong.

SAMPLE: A roaming cell-phone call to a nearby city costs less than a non-roaming call to a distant city.

This statement is wrong, or false, since roaming calls are more expensive.

This is not a complete list of all possible question forms, although most of the others are variations of these common types. You will always get complete directions for answering questions. Be sure you understand *how* to mark your answers – ask questions until you do.

V. RECORDING YOUR ANSWERS

Computer terminals are used more and more today for many different kinds of exams.

For an examination with very few applicants, you may be told to record your answers in the test booklet itself. Separate answer sheets are much more common. If this separate answer sheet is to be scored by machine – and this is often the case – it is highly important that you mark your answers correctly in order to get credit.

An electronic scoring machine is often used in civil service offices because of the speed with which papers can be scored. Machine-scored answer sheets must be marked with a pencil, which will be given to you. This pencil has a high graphite content which responds to the electronic scoring machine. As a matter of fact, stray dots may register as answers, so do not let your pencil rest on the answer sheet while you are pondering the correct answer. Also, if your pencil lead breaks or is otherwise defective, ask for another.

Since the answer sheet will be dropped in a slot in the scoring machine, be careful not to bend the corners or get the paper crumpled.

The answer sheet normally has five vertical columns of numbers, with 30 numbers to a column. These numbers correspond to the question numbers in your test booklet. After each number, going across the page are four or five pairs of dotted lines. These short dotted lines have small letters or numbers above them. The first two pairs may also have a "T" or "F" above the letters. This indicates that the first two pairs only are to be used if the questions are of the true-false type. If the questions are multiple choice, disregard the "T" and "F" and pay attention only to the small letters or numbers.

Answer your questions in the manner of the sample that follows:

32. The largest city in the United States is
    A. Washington, D.C.
    B. New York City
    C. Chicago
    D. Detroit
    E. San Francisco

1) Choose the answer you think is best. (New York City is the largest, so "B" is correct.)
2) Find the row of dotted lines numbered the same as the question you are answering. (Find row number 32)
3) Find the pair of dotted lines corresponding to the answer. (Find the pair of lines under the mark "B.")
4) Make a solid black mark between the dotted lines.

VI. BEFORE THE TEST

Common sense will help you find procedures to follow to get ready for an examination. Too many of us, however, overlook these sensible measures. Indeed, nervousness and fatigue have been found to be the most serious reasons why applicants fail to do their best on civil service tests. Here is a list of reminders:

- Begin your preparation early – Don't wait until the last minute to go scurrying around for books and materials or to find out what the position is all about.
- Prepare continuously – An hour a night for a week is better than an all-night cram session. This has been definitely established. What is more, a night a week for a month will return better dividends than crowding your study into a shorter period of time.
- Locate the place of the exam – You have been sent a notice telling you when and where to report for the examination. If the location is in a different town or otherwise unfamiliar to you, it would be well to inquire the best route and learn something about the building.
- Relax the night before the test – Allow your mind to rest. Do not study at all that night. Plan some mild recreation or diversion; then go to bed early and get a good night's sleep.
- Get up early enough to make a leisurely trip to the place for the test – This way unforeseen events, traffic snarls, unfamiliar buildings, etc. will not upset you.
- Dress comfortably – A written test is not a fashion show. You will be known by number and not by name, so wear something comfortable.

- Leave excess paraphernalia at home – Shopping bags and odd bundles will get in your way. You need bring only the items mentioned in the official notice you received; usually everything you need is provided. Do not bring reference books to the exam. They will only confuse those last minutes and be taken away from you when in the test room.
- Arrive somewhat ahead of time – If because of transportation schedules you must get there very early, bring a newspaper or magazine to take your mind off yourself while waiting.
- Locate the examination room – When you have found the proper room, you will be directed to the seat or part of the room where you will sit. Sometimes you are given a sheet of instructions to read while you are waiting. Do not fill out any forms until you are told to do so; just read them and be prepared.
- Relax and prepare to listen to the instructions
- If you have any physical problem that may keep you from doing your best, be sure to tell the test administrator. If you are sick or in poor health, you really cannot do your best on the exam. You can come back and take the test some other time.

VII. AT THE TEST

The day of the test is here and you have the test booklet in your hand. The temptation to get going is very strong. Caution! There is more to success than knowing the right answers. You must know how to identify your papers and understand variations in the type of short-answer question used in this particular examination. Follow these suggestions for maximum results from your efforts:

1) Cooperate with the monitor
The test administrator has a duty to create a situation in which you can be as much at ease as possible. He will give instructions, tell you when to begin, check to see that you are marking your answer sheet correctly, and so on. He is not there to guard you, although he will see that your competitors do not take unfair advantage. He wants to help you do your best.

2) Listen to all instructions
Don't jump the gun! Wait until you understand all directions. In most civil service tests you get more time than you need to answer the questions. So don't be in a hurry. Read each word of instructions until you clearly understand the meaning. Study the examples, listen to all announcements and follow directions. Ask questions if you do not understand what to do.

3) Identify your papers
Civil service exams are usually identified by number only. You will be assigned a number; you must not put your name on your test papers. Be sure to copy your number correctly. Since more than one exam may be given, copy your exact examination title.

4) Plan your time
Unless you are told that a test is a "speed" or "rate of work" test, speed itself is usually not important. Time enough to answer all the questions will be provided, but this does not mean that you have all day. An overall time limit has been set. Divide the total time (in minutes) by the number of questions to determine the approximate time you have for each question.

5) Do not linger over difficult questions

If you come across a difficult question, mark it with a paper clip (useful to have along) and come back to it when you have been through the booklet. One caution if you do this – be sure to skip a number on your answer sheet as well. Check often to be sure that you have not lost your place and that you are marking in the row numbered the same as the question you are answering.

6) Read the questions

Be sure you know what the question asks! Many capable people are unsuccessful because they failed to *read* the questions correctly.

7) Answer all questions

Unless you have been instructed that a penalty will be deducted for incorrect answers, it is better to guess than to omit a question.

8) Speed tests

It is often better NOT to guess on speed tests. It has been found that on timed tests people are tempted to spend the last few seconds before time is called in marking answers at random – without even reading them – in the hope of picking up a few extra points. To discourage this practice, the instructions may warn you that your score will be "corrected" for guessing. That is, a penalty will be applied. The incorrect answers will be deducted from the correct ones, or some other penalty formula will be used.

9) Review your answers

If you finish before time is called, go back to the questions you guessed or omitted to give them further thought. Review other answers if you have time.

10) Return your test materials

If you are ready to leave before others have finished or time is called, take ALL your materials to the monitor and leave quietly. Never take any test material with you. The monitor can discover whose papers are not complete, and taking a test booklet may be grounds for disqualification.

VIII. EXAMINATION TECHNIQUES

1) Read the general instructions carefully. These are usually printed on the first page of the exam booklet. As a rule, these instructions refer to the timing of the examination; the fact that you should not start work until the signal and must stop work at a signal, etc. If there are any *special* instructions, such as a choice of questions to be answered, make sure that you note this instruction carefully.

2) When you are ready to start work on the examination, that is as soon as the signal has been given, read the instructions to each question booklet, underline any key words or phrases, such as *least, best, outline, describe* and the like. In this way you will tend to answer as requested rather than discover on reviewing your paper that you *listed without describing*, that you selected the *worst* choice rather than the *best* choice, etc.

3) If the examination is of the objective or multiple-choice type – that is, each question will also give a series of possible answers: A, B, C or D, and you are called upon to select the best answer and write the letter next to that answer on your answer paper – it is advisable to start answering each question in turn. There may be anywhere from 50 to 100 such questions in the three or four hours allotted and you can see how much time would be taken if you read through all the questions before beginning to answer any. Furthermore, if you come across a question or group of questions which you know would be difficult to answer, it would undoubtedly affect your handling of all the other questions.

4) If the examination is of the essay type and contains but a few questions, it is a moot point as to whether you should read all the questions before starting to answer any one. Of course, if you are given a choice – say five out of seven and the like – then it is essential to read all the questions so you can eliminate the two that are most difficult. If, however, you are asked to answer all the questions, there may be danger in trying to answer the easiest one first because you may find that you will spend too much time on it. The best technique is to answer the first question, then proceed to the second, etc.

5) Time your answers. Before the exam begins, write down the time it started, then add the time allowed for the examination and write down the time it must be completed, then divide the time available somewhat as follows:
    - If 3-1/2 hours are allowed, that would be 210 minutes. If you have 80 objective-type questions, that would be an average of 2-1/2 minutes per question. Allow yourself no more than 2 minutes per question, or a total of 160 minutes, which will permit about 50 minutes to review.
    - If for the time allotment of 210 minutes there are 7 essay questions to answer, that would average about 30 minutes a question. Give yourself only 25 minutes per question so that you have about 35 minutes to review.

6) The most important instruction is to *read each question* and make sure you know what is wanted. The second most important instruction is to *time yourself properly* so that you answer every question. The third most important instruction is to *answer every question*. Guess if you have to but include something for each question. Remember that you will receive no credit for a blank and will probably receive some credit if you write something in answer to an essay question. If you guess a letter – say "B" for a multiple-choice question – you may have guessed right. If you leave a blank as an answer to a multiple-choice question, the examiners may respect your feelings but it will not add a point to your score. Some exams may penalize you for wrong answers, so in such cases *only*, you may not want to guess unless you have some basis for your answer.

7) Suggestions
    a. Objective-type questions
        1. Examine the question booklet for proper sequence of pages and questions
        2. Read all instructions carefully
        3. Skip any question which seems too difficult; return to it after all other questions have been answered
        4. Apportion your time properly; do not spend too much time on any single question or group of questions

5. Note and underline key words – *all, most, fewest, least, best, worst, same, opposite,* etc.
6. Pay particular attention to negatives
7. Note unusual option, e.g., unduly long, short, complex, different or similar in content to the body of the question
8. Observe the use of "hedging" words – *probably, may, most likely,* etc.
9. Make sure that your answer is put next to the same number as the question
10. Do not second-guess unless you have good reason to believe the second answer is definitely more correct
11. Cross out original answer if you decide another answer is more accurate; do not erase until you are ready to hand your paper in
12. Answer all questions; guess unless instructed otherwise
13. Leave time for review

b. Essay questions
1. Read each question carefully
2. Determine exactly what is wanted. Underline key words or phrases.
3. Decide on outline or paragraph answer
4. Include many different points and elements unless asked to develop any one or two points or elements
5. Show impartiality by giving pros and cons unless directed to select one side only
6. Make and write down any assumptions you find necessary to answer the questions
7. Watch your English, grammar, punctuation and choice of words
8. Time your answers; don't crowd material

8) Answering the essay question

Most essay questions can be answered by framing the specific response around several key words or ideas. Here are a few such key words or ideas:

M's: manpower, materials, methods, money, management
P's: purpose, program, policy, plan, procedure, practice, problems, pitfalls, personnel, public relations

a. Six basic steps in handling problems:
1. Preliminary plan and background development
2. Collect information, data and facts
3. Analyze and interpret information, data and facts
4. Analyze and develop solutions as well as make recommendations
5. Prepare report and sell recommendations
6. Install recommendations and follow up effectiveness

b. Pitfalls to avoid
1. *Taking things for granted* – A statement of the situation does not necessarily imply that each of the elements is necessarily true; for example, a complaint may be invalid and biased so that all that can be taken for granted is that a complaint has been registered

2. *Considering only one side of a situation* – Wherever possible, indicate several alternatives and then point out the reasons you selected the best one
3. *Failing to indicate follow up* – Whenever your answer indicates action on your part, make certain that you will take proper follow-up action to see how successful your recommendations, procedures or actions turn out to be
4. *Taking too long in answering any single question* – Remember to time your answers properly

IX. AFTER THE TEST

Scoring procedures differ in detail among civil service jurisdictions although the general principles are the same. Whether the papers are hand-scored or graded by machine we have described, they are nearly always graded by number. That is, the person who marks the paper knows only the number – never the name – of the applicant. Not until all the papers have been graded will they be matched with names. If other tests, such as training and experience or oral interview ratings have been given, scores will be combined. Different parts of the examination usually have different weights. For example, the written test might count 60 percent of the final grade, and a rating of training and experience 40 percent. In many jurisdictions, veterans will have a certain number of points added to their grades.

After the final grade has been determined, the names are placed in grade order and an eligible list is established. There are various methods for resolving ties between those who get the same final grade – probably the most common is to place first the name of the person whose application was received first. Job offers are made from the eligible list in the order the names appear on it. You will be notified of your grade and your rank as soon as all these computations have been made. This will be done as rapidly as possible.

People who are found to meet the requirements in the announcement are called "eligibles." Their names are put on a list of eligible candidates. An eligible's chances of getting a job depend on how high he stands on this list and how fast agencies are filling jobs from the list.

When a job is to be filled from a list of eligibles, the agency asks for the names of people on the list of eligibles for that job. When the civil service commission receives this request, it sends to the agency the names of the three people highest on this list. Or, if the job to be filled has specialized requirements, the office sends the agency the names of the top three persons who meet these requirements from the general list.

The appointing officer makes a choice from among the three people whose names were sent to him. If the selected person accepts the appointment, the names of the others are put back on the list to be considered for future openings.

That is the rule in hiring from all kinds of eligible lists, whether they are for typist, carpenter, chemist, or something else. For every vacancy, the appointing officer has his choice of any one of the top three eligibles on the list. This explains why the person whose name is on top of the list sometimes does not get an appointment when some of the persons lower on the list do. If the appointing officer chooses the second or third eligible, the No. 1 eligible does not get a job at once, but stays on the list until he is appointed or the list is terminated.

X. HOW TO PASS THE INTERVIEW TEST

The examination for which you applied requires an oral interview test. You have already taken the written test and you are now being called for the interview test – the final part of the formal examination.

You may think that it is not possible to prepare for an interview test and that there are no procedures to follow during an interview. Our purpose is to point out some things you can do in advance that will help you and some good rules to follow and pitfalls to avoid while you are being interviewed.

What is an interview supposed to test?

The written examination is designed to test the technical knowledge and competence of the candidate; the oral is designed to evaluate intangible qualities, not readily measured otherwise, and to establish a list showing the relative fitness of each candidate – as measured against his competitors – for the position sought. Scoring is not on the basis of "right" and "wrong," but on a sliding scale of values ranging from "not passable" to "outstanding." As a matter of fact, it is possible to achieve a relatively low score without a single "incorrect" answer because of evident weakness in the qualities being measured.

Occasionally, an examination may consist entirely of an oral test – either an individual or a group oral. In such cases, information is sought concerning the technical knowledges and abilities of the candidate, since there has been no written examination for this purpose. More commonly, however, an oral test is used to supplement a written examination.

Who conducts interviews?

The composition of oral boards varies among different jurisdictions. In nearly all, a representative of the personnel department serves as chairman. One of the members of the board may be a representative of the department in which the candidate would work. In some cases, "outside experts" are used, and, frequently, a businessman or some other representative of the general public is asked to serve. Labor and management or other special groups may be represented. The aim is to secure the services of experts in the appropriate field.

However the board is composed, it is a good idea (and not at all improper or unethical) to ascertain in advance of the interview who the members are and what groups they represent. When you are introduced to them, you will have some idea of their backgrounds and interests, and at least you will not stutter and stammer over their names.

What should be done before the interview?

While knowledge about the board members is useful and takes some of the surprise element out of the interview, there is other preparation which is more substantive. It *is* possible to prepare for an oral interview – in several ways:

1) Keep a copy of your application and review it carefully before the interview

This may be the only document before the oral board, and the starting point of the interview. Know what education and experience you have listed there, and the sequence and dates of all of it. Sometimes the board will ask you to review the highlights of your experience for them; you should not have to hem and haw doing it.

2) Study the class specification and the examination announcement

Usually, the oral board has one or both of these to guide them. The qualities, characteristics or knowledges required by the position sought are stated in these documents. They offer valuable clues as to the nature of the oral interview. For example, if the job involves supervisory responsibilities, the announcement will usually indicate that knowledge of modern supervisory methods and the qualifications of the candidate as a supervisor will be tested. If so, you can expect such questions, frequently in the form of a hypothetical situation which you are expected to solve. NEVER go into an oral without knowledge of the duties and responsibilities of the job you seek.

3) Think through each qualification required

Try to visualize the kind of questions you would ask if you were a board member. How well could you answer them? Try especially to appraise your own knowledge and background in each area, *measured against the job sought*, and identify any areas in which you are weak. Be critical and realistic – do not flatter yourself.

4) Do some general reading in areas in which you feel you may be weak

For example, if the job involves supervision and your past experience has NOT, some general reading in supervisory methods and practices, particularly in the field of human relations, might be useful. Do NOT study agency procedures or detailed manuals. The oral board will be testing your understanding and capacity, not your memory.

5) Get a good night's sleep and watch your general health and mental attitude

You will want a clear head at the interview. Take care of a cold or any other minor ailment, and of course, no hangovers.

What should be done on the day of the interview?

Now comes the day of the interview itself. Give yourself plenty of time to get there. Plan to arrive somewhat ahead of the scheduled time, particularly if your appointment is in the fore part of the day. If a previous candidate fails to appear, the board might be ready for you a bit early. By early afternoon an oral board is almost invariably behind schedule if there are many candidates, and you may have to wait. Take along a book or magazine to read, or your application to review, but leave any extraneous material in the waiting room when you go in for your interview. In any event, relax and compose yourself.

The matter of dress is important. The board is forming impressions about you – from your experience, your manners, your attitude, and your appearance. Give your personal appearance careful attention. Dress your best, but not your flashiest. Choose conservative, appropriate clothing, and be sure it is immaculate. This is a business interview, and your appearance should indicate that you regard it as such. Besides, being well groomed and properly dressed will help boost your confidence.

Sooner or later, someone will call your name and escort you into the interview room. *This is it.* From here on you are on your own. It is too late for any more preparation. But remember, you asked for this opportunity to prove your fitness, and you are here because your request was granted.

What happens when you go in?

The usual sequence of events will be as follows: The clerk (who is often the board stenographer) will introduce you to the chairman of the oral board, who will introduce you to the other members of the board. Acknowledge the introductions before you sit down. Do not be surprised if you find a microphone facing you or a stenotypist sitting by. Oral interviews are usually recorded in the event of an appeal or other review.

Usually the chairman of the board will open the interview by reviewing the highlights of your education and work experience from your application – primarily for the benefit of the other members of the board, as well as to get the material into the record. Do not interrupt or comment unless there is an error or significant misinterpretation; if that is the case, do not hesitate. But do not quibble about insignificant matters. Also, he will usually ask you some question about your education, experience or your present job – partly to get you to start talking and to establish the interviewing "rapport." He may start the actual questioning, or turn it over to one of the other members. Frequently, each member undertakes the questioning on a particular area, one in which he is perhaps most competent, so you can expect each member to participate in the examination. Because time is limited, you may also expect some rather abrupt switches in the direction the questioning takes, so do not be upset by it. Normally, a board member will not pursue a single line of questioning unless he discovers a particular strength or weakness.

After each member has participated, the chairman will usually ask whether any member has any further questions, then will ask you if you have anything you wish to add. Unless you are expecting this question, it may floor you. Worse, it may start you off on an extended, extemporaneous speech. The board is not usually seeking more information. The question is principally to offer you a last opportunity to present further qualifications or to indicate that you have nothing to add. So, if you feel that a significant qualification or characteristic has been overlooked, it is proper to point it out in a sentence or so. Do not compliment the board on the thoroughness of their examination – they have been sketchy, and you know it. If you wish, merely say, "No thank you, I have nothing further to add." This is a point where you can "talk yourself out" of a good impression or fail to present an important bit of information. Remember, *you close the interview yourself.*

The chairman will then say, "That is all, Mr. _____, thank you." Do not be startled; the interview is over, and quicker than you think. Thank him, gather your belongings and take your leave. Save your sigh of relief for the other side of the door.

How to put your best foot forward
Throughout this entire process, you may feel that the board individually and collectively is trying to pierce your defenses, seek out your hidden weaknesses and embarrass and confuse you. Actually, this is not true. They are obliged to make an appraisal of your qualifications for the job you are seeking, and they want to see you in your best light. Remember, they must interview all candidates and a non-cooperative candidate may become a failure in spite of their best efforts to bring out his qualifications. Here are 15 suggestions that will help you:

1) Be natural – Keep your attitude confident, not cocky
If you are not confident that you can do the job, do not expect the board to be. Do not apologize for your weaknesses, try to bring out your strong points. The board is interested in a positive, not negative, presentation. Cockiness will antagonize any board member and make him wonder if you are covering up a weakness by a false show of strength.

2) Get comfortable, but don't lounge or sprawl
Sit erectly but not stiffly. A careless posture may lead the board to conclude that you are careless in other things, or at least that you are not impressed by the importance of the occasion. Either conclusion is natural, even if incorrect. Do not fuss with your clothing, a pencil or an ashtray. Your hands may occasionally be useful to emphasize a point; do not let them become a point of distraction.

3) Do not wisecrack or make small talk
This is a serious situation, and your attitude should show that you consider it as such. Further, the time of the board is limited – they do not want to waste it, and neither should you.

4) Do not exaggerate your experience or abilities

In the first place, from information in the application or other interviews and sources, the board may know more about you than you think. Secondly, you probably will not get away with it. An experienced board is rather adept at spotting such a situation, so do not take the chance.

5) If you know a board member, do not make a point of it, yet do not hide it

Certainly you are not fooling him, and probably not the other members of the board. Do not try to take advantage of your acquaintanceship – it will probably do you little good.

6) Do not dominate the interview

Let the board do that. They will give you the clues – do not assume that you have to do all the talking. Realize that the board has a number of questions to ask you, and do not try to take up all the interview time by showing off your extensive knowledge of the answer to the first one.

7) Be attentive

You only have 20 minutes or so, and you should keep your attention at its sharpest throughout. When a member is addressing a problem or question to you, give him your undivided attention. Address your reply principally to him, but do not exclude the other board members.

8) Do not interrupt

A board member may be stating a problem for you to analyze. He will ask you a question when the time comes. Let him state the problem, and wait for the question.

9) Make sure you understand the question

Do not try to answer until you are sure what the question is. If it is not clear, restate it in your own words or ask the board member to clarify it for you. However, do not haggle about minor elements.

10) Reply promptly but not hastily

A common entry on oral board rating sheets is "candidate responded readily," or "candidate hesitated in replies." Respond as promptly and quickly as you can, but do not jump to a hasty, ill-considered answer.

11) Do not be peremptory in your answers

A brief answer is proper – but do not fire your answer back. That is a losing game from your point of view. The board member can probably ask questions much faster than you can answer them.

12) Do not try to create the answer you think the board member wants

He is interested in what kind of mind you have and how it works – not in playing games. Furthermore, he can usually spot this practice and will actually grade you down on it.

13) Do not switch sides in your reply merely to agree with a board member

Frequently, a member will take a contrary position merely to draw you out and to see if you are willing and able to defend your point of view. Do not start a debate, yet do not surrender a good position. If a position is worth taking, it is worth defending.

14) Do not be afraid to admit an error in judgment if you are shown to be wrong

The board knows that you are forced to reply without any opportunity for careful consideration. Your answer may be demonstrably wrong. If so, admit it and get on with the interview.

15) Do not dwell at length on your present job

The opening question may relate to your present assignment. Answer the question but do not go into an extended discussion. You are being examined for a *new* job, not your present one. As a matter of fact, try to phrase ALL your answers in terms of the job for which you are being examined.

Basis of Rating

Probably you will forget most of these "do's" and "don'ts" when you walk into the oral interview room. Even remembering them all will not ensure you a passing grade. Perhaps you did not have the qualifications in the first place. But remembering them will help you to put your best foot forward, without treading on the toes of the board members.

Rumor and popular opinion to the contrary notwithstanding, an oral board wants you to make the best appearance possible. They know you are under pressure – but they also want to see how you respond to it as a guide to what your reaction would be under the pressures of the job you seek. They will be influenced by the degree of poise you display, the personal traits you show and the manner in which you respond.

ABOUT THIS BOOK

This book contains tests divided into Examination Sections. Go through each test, answering every question in the margin. We have also attached a sample answer sheet at the back of the book that can be removed and used. At the end of each test look at the answer key and check your answers. On the ones you got wrong, look at the right answer choice and learn. Do not fill in the answers first. Do not memorize the questions and answers, but understand the answer and principles involved. On your test, the questions will likely be different from the samples. Questions are changed and new ones added. If you understand these past questions you should have success with any changes that arise. Tests may consist of several types of questions. We have additional books on each subject should more study be advisable or necessary for you. Finally, the more you study, the better prepared you will be. This book is intended to be the last thing you study before you walk into the examination room. Prior study of relevant texts is also recommended. NLC publishes some of these in our Fundamental Series. Knowledge and good sense are important factors in passing your exam. Good luck also helps. So now study this Passbook, absorb the material contained within and take that knowledge into the examination. Then do your best to pass that exam.

EXAMINATION SECTION

EXAMINATION SECTION
TEST 1

DIRECTIONS: Each question or incomplete statement is followed by several suggested answers or completions. Select the one that BEST answers the question or completes the statement. *PRINT THE LETTER OF THE CORRECT ANSWER IN THE SPACE AT THE RIGHT.*

1. Which of the following municipal solid waste characteristics must a municipal waste collection operator be concerned with? 1.____

    A. Combustible materials content
    B. Chemical or elemental composition
    C. Moisture content, density, arrival time pattern
    D. All of the above

2. Oversized bulky waste is defined as being comprised of 2.____

    A. construction debris, excluding ash
    B. large furniture or appliances
    C. demolition debris, especially nonferrous content
    D. agricultural debris, such as sand or glass

3. Which of the following is a problem with the melting of aluminum and glass in furnaces? 3.____

    A. Blocks grate air passages
    B. Forms slag on economizer surfaces
    C. Increases SOx emissions
    D. Causes degradation of boiler tubes

4. Which of the following is a means of reducing nitrogen oxides in a furnace? 4.____

    A. Lime injection
    B. Chlorine injection
    C. Diverting yard waste from municipal solid waste
    D. Increasing excess air

5. Which of the following basic elements, when present in municipal solid waste, will form an acid gas in flue gases? 5.____

    A. Argon   B. Nitrogen   C. Chlorine   D. Ammonia

6. NO_x in the form of (NO or NO_2) can 6.____

    A. cause direct damage to plant materials
    B. create slag on boiler tubes
    C. form nitric acid and smog
    D. all of the above

7. Trace metals such as lead can become an exposure hazard to personnel in contact with 7.____

    A. flue gases   B. excess air
    C. fly and bottom ash   D. air pollution monitoring equipment

1

8. What is the PRIMARY goal of environmental public relations? 8.____

   A. Divert potential lawsuits
   B. Calming environmental concerns
   C. Cover up a problem
   D. Manipulate the media

9. Which of the following are particulates carried by flue gases? 9.____

   A. Soot
   B. Unburnt material
   C. Fly ash
   D. All of the above

10. Particulates in flue gases contribute to 10.____

    A. reduced visibility (smog)
    B. Increased precipitation
    C. Respiratory problems
    D. All of the above

11. Which of the following is an advantage of baghouses over electrostatic precipitators for particulate control? 11.____

    A. Less expensive
    B. Lower pressure drop
    C. Collects more particulates
    D. No temperature limitations

12. Which of the following affect the efficiency of a bag-house? 12.____

    A. Type of fabric used in bags
    B. Efficiency of cleaning
    C. Amount of leaks around bags
    D. All of the above

13. Underfire air should be adjusted to match 13.____

    A. total oxygen
    B. total CO
    C. refuse bed depth in furnace
    D. grate speed

14. Which of the following controls NO_x emissions? 14.____

    A. Increased furnace temperatures
    B. Higher excess air ratios
    C. Injection of ammonia
    D. All of the above

15. In a wet scrubber, sulfur dioxides are removed by 15.____

    A. vaporization
    B. oxidation
    C. absorption
    D. impingement

16. Which of the following contribute to the energy of a fluid in a pipe?

    A. Velocity, head pressure
    B. Friction, temperature, viscosity
    C. Pipe size, pressure, temperature
    D. Fluid type, density, specific gravity

16.____

17. Static head is defined as

    A. elevation of the process fluid above reference point
    B. flow of the fluid in the pipe
    C. resistance of the pipe to flow of fluid
    D. all of the above

17.____

18. Which of the following is NOT true of a typical positive displacement pump?

    A. Has a head capacity curve with a zero flow point
    B. Cannot be operated with discharge/recirc valves both shut
    C. Commonly used for metering pumps
    D. Will continue to pump as system discharge pressure rises

18.____

19. Which type of valve is used for basic shut off or isolation?

    A. Gate   B. Globe   C. Throttle   D. Plug

19.____

20. A _____ valve would be used to ensure flow in one direction.

    A. swing-check   B. plug
    C. butterfly   D. relief

20.____

21. Which of the following systems would have a safety valve instead of a relief valve?

    A. Water   B. Oil
    C. Steam   D. All of the above

21.____

22. Lubricants

    A. reduce corrosion oh metal components
    B. have no cooling effect on metals
    C. act only to reduce friction and resistance
    D. break down into inert elements

22.____

23. The effective maintenance of systems can reduce the costs of

    A. keeping equipment operating
    B. maintaining backup equipment
    C. revenue lost due to excessive plant shutdowns
    D. all of the above

23.____

24. Vibration analysis, lube oil sample analysis, and ultrasonic testing are examples of _____ maintenance.

    A. preventative   B. predictive
    C. corrective   D. indicative

24.____

25. A storeroom inventory system determines proper inventory A storeroom inventory system determines proper inventory levels by

    A. evaluating stocking levels relative to demand
    B. avoiding losses due to thefts
    C. maintaining up-to-date parts
    D. all of the above

25.____

KEY (CORRECT ANSWERS)

1.	D	11.	C
2.	B	12.	D
3.	A	13.	C
4.	C	14.	C
5.	C	15.	C
6.	C	16.	A
7.	C	17.	A
8.	B	18.	A
9.	D	19.	A
10.	D	20.	A

21. C
22. A
23. D
24. B
25. D

TEST 2

DIRECTIONS: Each question or incomplete statement is followed by several suggested answers or completions. Select the one that BEST answers the question or completes the statement. *PRINT THE LETTER OF THE CORRECT ANSWER IN THE SPACE AT THE RIGHT.*

1. Which of the following is NOT defined by New Source Performance Standards as municipal solid waste?

    A. Major automobile components
    B. Household discards
    C. Lead-acid batteries
    D. Yard wastes

2. The useful heating value of municipal solid waste is related to the

    A. combustible components of the ash
    B. density of the municipal solid waste
    C. percent of ash content of the municipal solid waste
    D. all of the above

3. Which of the following is a means of dealing with extra moist loads of municipal solid waste?

    A. *Fluffing* or mixing of municipal solid waste by crane/furnace feeder operator
    B. Reducing residence time of municipal solid waste on grate in furnace
    C. Minimizing acceptance of *wet trash* with excessive moisture content
    D. Maintaining furnace controls in auto mode to ensure complete burn

4. Which of the following is NOT true of refuse derived fuel (RDF)?

    A. Uniform combustion properties
    B. Is a type of municipal solid waste
    C. Relatively low in residue amount
    D. Relatively low BTU value

5. The amount of nitrogen oxides produced in a furnace is relative to

    A. operations at above normal furnace temperatures
    B. the amount of nitrogen content in the municipal solid waste
    C. the amount of excess air used
    D. all of the above

6. Proximate analysis of fuel provides information on

    A. heating value, volatility, ash content
    B. moisture content, specific gravity, vapor density
    C. sulfur content, pH, municipal solid waste rating
    D. flash point, pour point, viscosity

7. Which of the following is formed as a product of incomplete combustion?

    A. Carbon dioxide   B. Dioxins
    C. Nitrogen   D. Oxygen

8. Hazardous wastes are grouped as

   A. synthetic organics
   B. toxic wastes
   C. reactive metals
   D. all of the above

9. Which of the following is considered household hazardous waste (HHW)?

   A. Paint
   B. Pesticides
   C. Dry and wet cell batteries
   D. All of the above

10. A typical arrival time pattern of municipal solid waste finds tonnage at a peak flow at

    A. early morning hours
    B. late afternoon hours
    C. noon
    D. early afternoon hours

11. The BEST method to use for informing the press/media of events is by

    A. news releases
    B. internal memos
    C. interview plant personnel
    D. conduct periodic briefings

12. A secondary goal of public relations is to
    I. improve your image
    II. calm environmental concerns
    III. cover up a problem
    IV. manipulate the media
    The CORRECT answer is:

    A. I only   B. I, II   C. II, III   D. III, IV

13. Which of the following public relation tools is considered the MOST effective?

    A. Spin
    B. Press conference
    C. Media event
    D. Internal memo

14. What percent of all CO emissions are man made?

    A. 10%   B. 20%   C. 50%   D. 75%

15. Which of the following increases the velocity of flue gases in the bags of a baghouse?

    A. Running lower oxygen levels in the stack
    B. Underfiring the furnace
    C. Taking one or more sections of baghouse off line for cleaning
    D. All of the above

16. Refuse bed depth should be adjusted so that

    A. the largest depth is on initial grates
    B. it is even over all grates
    C. the largest depth is on final grates for burn off
    D. it is higher on middle grates for drying

17. Which of the following describes components in an electrostatic precipitator?   17.____

    A. Low voltage applied to vertical wires
    B. Use of oppositely charged horizontal plates
    C. Rappers or vibrators on plates and hopper
    D. None of the above

18. The control technique for control of organics is the same as for   18.____

    A. CO   B. HCl   C. NO_X D. SO_X

19. To determine static head of a pump, one must know the   19.____

    A. level of water into discharge tank from pump
    B. suction head
    C. suction lift
    D. level of water in supply tank to pump

20. Total dynamic head includes the following critical factors: 20.____

    A. Total static head, pipe friction, velocity head
    B. Total suction head, fluid velocity, pipe head loss
    C. Total static head, total suction lift, pipe head loss
    D. Fluid temperature, fluid pressure, fluid density

21. Which of the following is a component of a centrifugal pump?   21.____

    A. Lobe   B. Volute
    C. Piston   D. Crankshaft

22. Which of the following types of centrifugal pumps has an angular flow of fluid through its   22.____
    impeller?

    A. Radial   B. Mixed flow
    C. Axial   D. Single flow

23. Which of the following types of centrifugal pumps would be used in a high discharge   23.____
    head application?

    A. Mixed flow   B. Radial
    C. Propeller   D. Axial

24. Preventative maintenance includes   24.____

    A. inspections
    B. lubrication
    C. replacement of equipment
    D. all of the above

25. Excessive preventive maintenance can   25.____

    A. increase availability of equipment
    B. permit better planning of maintenance efforts
    C. increase operation and maintenance costs
    D. increase equipment reliability

KEY (CORRECT ANSWERS)

1. A
2. C
3. A
4. D
5. D

6. A
7. B
8. D
9. D
10. C

11. B
12. A
13. D
14. B
15. C

16. B
17. C
18. A
19. A
20. A

21. B
22. B
23. B
24. D
25. C

EXAMINATION SECTION
TEST 1

DIRECTIONS: Each question or incomplete statement is followed by several suggested answers or completions. Select the one that BEST answers the question or completes the statement. *PRINT THE LETTER OF THE CORRECT ANSWER IN THE SPACE AT THE RIGHT.*

1. Of the following, the LARGEST constituent component of average municipal solid waste (based on weight) is

    A. yard wastes
    B. glass and metal
    C. paper and cardboard
    D. miscellaneous

    1.____

2. Of the following, which is a chemical element in municipal solid waste?

    A. Volatile matter
    B. Sulfur
    C. Paper and cardboard
    D. Water

    2.____

3. Of the following, the component material in municipal solid waste which has an organic composition is

    A. aluminum
    B. pottery
    C. glass
    D. fixed carbon

    3.____

4. Which of the following items is NOT included in the proximate analysis?

    A. Volatile matter
    B. Hydrogen
    C. Fixed carbon
    D. Moisture

    4.____

5. _____ wastes are NOT a source of municipal solid waste.

    A. Industrial
    B. Household
    C. Commercial
    D. Institutional

    5.____

6. The total amount of municipal solid waste delivered to municipal waste collection facilities is GENERALLY at a minimum during the

    A. spring   B. summer   C. fall   D. winter

    6.____

7. The moisture content in municipal solid waste is HIGHEST

    A. just after a rain
    B. on Mondays because of weekend yard work
    C. after a holiday when there is no pickup
    D. all of the above

    7.____

8. Until the recent initiatives for recycling, the average individual in industrial communities produced _____ municipal solid waste as/than those in rural areas.

    A. about the same
    B. more
    C. less
    D. it cannot be determined

    8.____

9. The PRIMARY reason behind the increased public scrutiny about ash disposal practices is its concern about

   A. metals recycling
   B. heavy metals leaching into the groundwater
   C. jobs
   D. recycling everything

10. Under current Resource Conservation and Recovery Act requirements, in the design of sanitary landfills, it is NOT required to use a

    A. double liner
    B. leachate collection system
    C. leachate monitoring system
    D. methane gas powered electric generator system

11. Composting is an important factor for municipal waste collection unit operations because it

    A. removes materials from the waste which tend to burn poorly and increase nitrogen oxide emissions
    B. is the cheapest way to handle wastes
    C. makes a lot of money
    D. all of the above

12. The MOST important public relations characteristic of an operator is that he be

    A. trustworthy   B. a sharp looker
    C. college educated   D. a good speaker

13. The Clean Air Act

    A. allows the states to establish municipal waste collection regulations that are stricter than the federal standards
    B. prohibits the states from having municipal waste collection regulations that are stricter than the federal standard
    C. sets the maximum regulatory limit on municipal waste collection emission standards
    D. does not allow the consideration of economics in the setting of new source performance standards

14. In the _____, Congress authorized the Environmental Protection Agency to require the states to regulate existing municipal waste collection units.

    A. Standards of Performance for New Stationary Sources, Municipal Waste Collections
    B. Comprehensive Environmental Response Compensation and Liability Act
    C. Clean Air Act
    D. State Implementation Plan Act

15. The Clean Air Act requires each state to submit plans for implementing air pollution control and the Environmental Protection Agency to review and approve them.
    If this is not done, the state will be under threat of

A. losing their ability to regulate air pollutants
B. losing all federal highway funds
C. attracting less industry
D. all of the above

16. The Environmental Protection Agency New Source Performance Standard for new municipal waste collection units does NOT require regulation of

    A. carbon monoxide
    B. carbon dioxide
    C. nitric oxides
    D. dioxins and furans

16._____

17. The municipal solid waste characteristic that is UNACCEPTABLE at all municipal waste collection facilities is

    A. batteries
    B. medical waste discards
    C. tires
    D. radioactive wastes

17._____

18. Explosions at municipal waste collections can be caused by

    A. explosive munitions
    B. gas cylinders
    C. liquid drums of solvents
    D. all of the above

18._____

19. Of the following, the element of an integrated solid waste management system which can result in lowering the toxicity of manufactured materials is

    A. incineration
    B. recycling
    C. landfill
    D. source reduction

19._____

20. Of the following, the element of an integrated solid waste management system which will lower the metals and glass composition in municipal solid waste at the municipal waste collection is

    A. incineration
    B. recycling
    C. landfill
    D. source reduction

20._____

21. The element of an integrated solid waste management system which is generally considered to include composting is

    A. incineration
    B. recycling
    C. landfill
    D. source reduction

21._____

22. The recycling program activity which can reduce the potential quantity of formation of municipal waste collection acid gases is _____ removal.

    A. metal
    B. glass
    C. paper
    D. plastic

22._____

23. An average higher heating value of the municipal solid waste is APPROXIMATELY _____ Btu/lbm.

    A. 3,000
    B. 5,000
    C. 7,000
    D. 9,000

23._____

24. In general, the higher heating value of a large mass of municipal solid waste can vary from 2,000 Btu/lbm to maximum of about _____ Btu/lbm, depending upon how much mixing occurs and what is being charged.

    A. 3,000
    B. 8,000
    C. 25,000
    D. 50,000

24._____

25. The PRIMARY activity of a(n) _____ is to separate the light fluff fractions of municipal solid waste from the heavier non-combustible grit and glass.   25.____

    A. Trommel screen
    B. shredder
    C. flail mill
    D. air classifier

KEY (CORRECT ANSWERS)

1.	C	11.	A
2.	B	12.	A
3.	D	13.	A
4.	B	14.	C
5.	A	15.	D
6.	D	16.	B
7.	D	17.	A
8.	B	18.	D
9.	B	19.	D
10.	D	20.	B

21. C
22. D
23. B
24. B
25. D

TEST 2

DIRECTIONS: Each question or incomplete statement is followed by several suggested answers or completions. Select the one that BEST answers the question or completes the statement. *PRINT THE LETTER OF THE CORRECT ANSWER IN THE SPACE AT THE RIGHT.*

1. The PRIMARY activity of a(n) _____ is to reduce the size of municipal solid waste pieces to around 2.5 inches across. 1.____

   A. Trommel screen B. shredder
   C. flail mill D. air classifier

2. A population of 1,000,000 people on average produces about _____ tons of municipal solid waste per day. 2.____

   A. 350 B. 1,000 C. 1,700 D. 3,500

3. The APPROXIMATE stoichiometric amount of air, in pounds, required to burn a pound of average municipal solid waste is 3.____

   A. 0.5 B. 3 C. 6 D. 15

4. The typical amount of air supplied in a municipal waste collection unit for burning each pound of solid waste is about _____ pounds. 4.____

   A. 0.5 B. 3 C. 6 D. 12

5. A refractory coating on the waterwall surfaces below the over fire air ports will 5.____

   A. reflect more of the radiant energy back to the combustion zone
   B. reduce the amount of heat extraction from the waterwalls
   C. cause higher combustion gas temperatures
   D. all of the above

6. The air flow control device which provides the GREATEST precision of control on the air flow rate would be 6.____

   A. inlet vane dampers on a FD fan
   B. duct dampers
   C. variable speed driven motors on the fans
   D. all of the above

7. A properly operating *in situ* monitor indicates 200 ppm of SO_2 in the flue gas when the moisture in the flue gas is known to be 15%. 7.____
   If an extractive instrument which has an in-line dryer indicates 235 ppm of SO_2, then the

   A. two instruments are reading consistently
   B. extractive instrument is reading too high
   C. extractive instrument is reading too low
   D. none of the above

8. Properly operating extractive CEMS instruments indicate 200 ppm of SO_2 and 9% oxygen in the flue gas.
   The standard emission concentration of SO_2 corrected to 7% flue gas oxygen would be _____ ppm of SO_2.

   A. 200
   B. greater than 200
   C. less than 200
   D. none of the above

9. The uncontrolled particulate emissions in the flue gas (at the entrance to the APCD) from modular, starved air incinerators is about _____ that of conventional grate firing, mass burn systems.

   A. half   B. twice   C. ten times   D. one-tenth

10. The overall amount of excess air used in refuse derived fuel fired municipal waste collections is about _____ that of conventional grate firing, mass burn systems.

    A. the same as
    B. 25 percent more than
    C. 25 percent less than
    D. twice as much as

11. The New Source Performance Standard for new municipal waste collections sets an upper limit on the temperature of the flue gas entering the air pollution control device. The limit was established to

    A. assure that there would be no condensation of flue gas in the APCD
    B. minimize formation of dioxin/furan compounds
    C. maximize the APCD particulate collection efficiency
    D. assure that there would not be any fires in the ESP or baghouse

12. Mercury emissions are a particular problem for combustion systems such as municipal waste collections because

    A. the municipal waste collection combustion environment provides unique conditions for vaporizing mercury
    B. mercury has a very high vapor pressure, even at relatively low temperatures
    C. mercury causes ash particulates to become sticky
    D. mercury substantially increases the weight of municipal waste collection ash

13. Which of the following statements about NO_X emissions from municipal waste collection systems is NOT correct?

    A. The temperature levels are too low to cause significant levels of thermal NO_x formation.
    B. The majority of the NOx is emitted as NO_2.
    C. The dominant source of NO_X formation is oxidation of nitrogen in the fuel.
    D. Flue gas recirculation will not be an effective NO_X control technique for municipal waste collections.

14. Carbon monoxide emission concentration is an indication to the operator and regulator of the

    A. overall combustion efficiency in the boiler
    B. color of the plume

C. temperature on the grate
D. quality of the bottom ash

15. A main concern about municipal waste collections which led to the development of new air emissions standards was the release of dioxin/furan emissions. Since these pollutants are toxic compounds, the Environmental Protection Agency had congressional authority to regulate municipal waste collection emissions by establishing a national emission standard for hazardous air pollutant (NESHAP).
If the Environmental Protection Agency had used that authority, which of the following statements would be TRUE?

   A. Regulations could be applied only to new units.
   B. Economic impact would be a consideration in setting the emission limits.
   C. The same emission limits would apply to both new and existing municipal waste collections.
   D. Different emission limits could be established for different classes of municipal waste collections.

16. In any combustion system, a portion of the inorganic material in the flue will be released as fly ash. For a pulverized coal fired utility boiler, about 80% of the ash leaves the boiler as fly ash.
The percentage of the fuel ash which leaves a refuse derived fuel facility as fly ash is APPROXIMATELY _____ %.

   A. 60-80   B. 40-60   C. 20-40   D. 10-20

17. In any combustion system, a portion of the inorganic material in the flue will be released as fly ash. For a pulverized coal fired utility boiler, about 80% of the ash leaves the boiler as fly ash. The percentage of the fuel ash which leaves a modular starved air facility as fly ash is APPROXIMATELY _____ %.

   A. 40-60   B. 20-40
   C. 10-20   D. less than 5

18. Refuse derived fuel systems use travelling grates because

   A. refuse derived fuel pieces are so small that they would jam up the air passageways if burned on pusher grates
   B. refuse derived fuel requires a thin fuel bed to prevent particulate entrainment
   C. since about half the refuse derived fuel burns in suspension, the refuse derived fuel on the grate does not clump up and need the physical bed mixing to provide air
   D. refuse derived fuel has more aluminum and glass than mass burned municipal solid waste, which makes clinkering on the fuel bed a more serious problem

19. When underfire air blows through the bed of municipal solid waste on a grate or hearth, the burning process GENERALLY proceeds

   A. from the hearth up
   B. from the top surface down toward the grate
   C. as a uniformly distributed flame condition throughout the entire bed
   D. according to the composition of the municipal solid waste

20. The combustion efficiency of a modern, water-wall municipal waste collection unit based on the overall utilization of carbon is

    A. about 25-40%
    B. about 70-85%
    C. about 85-95%
    D. greater than 95%

21. The combustion efficiency of a modern, water-wall municipal waste collection unit based on fuel energy to steam production is

    A. about 25-40%
    B. about 70-85%
    C. about 90-99%
    D. greater than 99%

22. Designers of municipal waste collections generally limit the steam temperatures to around 800F and the pressure to around 800 psia because

    A. unit efficiency is greater at high pressures and temperatures
    B. to go to higher temperatures and pressures would increase the cost of the pumps
    C. of concern about chloride corrosion in the superheater
    D. it is easier to maintain temperature and pressures at these values

23. Soot blowing is accomplished on a routine basis to

    A. keep a proper cake loading on the air pollution control devices
    B. blow off slag from the furnace walls
    C. to remove ash build-up from the tube surfaces in the convection section
    D. discharge excess steam produced in the boiler

24. Which of the following is an example of a negative pressure facemask?

    A. Constant supply of air is directed into the mask.
    B. Upon inhaling, air is drawn in through regulator or filters.
    C. Air passes from the inside of the mask to the outside.
    D. All of the above

25. A turbine/generator is running on load control. A sudden increase in load will cause _____ in the boiler steam drums.

    A. shrinking
    B. swelling
    C. foaming
    D. thermal stress

KEY (CORRECT ANSWERS)

1.	B	11.	B
2.	C	12.	B
3.	B	13.	B
4.	C	14.	A
5.	D	15.	C
6.	C	16.	D
7.	A	17.	D
8.	B	18.	C
9.	D	19.	B
10.	C	20.	D

21. B
22. C
23. C
24. B
25. B

EXAMINATION SECTION
TEST 1

DIRECTIONS: Each question or incomplete statement is followed by several suggested answers or completions. Select the one that BEST answers the question or completes the statement. *PRINT THE LETTER OF THE CORRECT ANSWER IN THE SPACE AT THE RIGHT.*

1. The GREATEST percentage by weight in the refuse stream is constituted by

    A. metals
    B. ash
    C. paper products
    D. wood

    1.____

2. Municipal solid waste is BEST characterized by its

    A. homogeneity
    B. inconsistency
    C. high BTU value
    D. low entropy

    2.____

3. Combustion air fans should be started in which order?

    A. ID, secondary, primary
    B. Secondary, primary, ID
    C. ID, burner fans, primary
    D. ID, primary, secondary

    3.____

4. If you were operating in manual, and you opened the ID fan dampers, the pressure in the furnace would IMMEDIATELY

    A. decrease
    B. increase
    C. not be affected
    D. increase then decrease

    4.____

5. In what position should a fan's dampers be when the fan is started?

    A. Open
    B. Closed
    C. Halfway open
    D. Slightly cracked open

    5.____

6. What is the PRIMARY concern when maintaining equipment?

    A. Safety
    B. The life of the equipment
    C. Cost
    D. Production

    6.____

7. The last point of air injection in the furnace is called _____ air.

    A. primary
    B. combustion
    C. secondary
    D. draft

    7.____

8. The cause of a short-lived vibration and rumble in your turbine would MOST likely be that the

    A. oil wedge broke
    B. water entered the blading
    C. bearing is shot
    D. steam safeties blew

    8.____

9. Lockout can be requested by

    A. the board operator
    B. the plant manager
    C. the maintenance operator
    D. anyone involved in the work

    9.____

10. What is the turbine acceleration rate if a turbine goes from 500 rpm to 3600 rpm in 11 minutes?

    A. 282 rpm/m
    B. 300 rpm/m
    C. 6200 rpm/s
    D. 10000 rpm/s

11. The purpose of a feedwater regulating valve is to

    A. restrict water flow
    B. control the level in the deaerator
    C. control the level in the condenser
    D. take water flows and levels into account and supply enough water to the steam drum

12. The drain at normal operating level in the steam drum is called the

    A. emergency blowdown
    B. continuous blowdown
    C. feedwater supply line
    D. chemical feed line

13. A boiler is purged to

    A. remove possible build-up of combustible gases
    B. supply plenty of oxygen to the furnace for combustion
    C. establish boiler draft
    D. ensure fan-ready status

14. What are the three combustible chemical elements?

    A. Carbon, hydrogen, and sulfur
    B. Sulfur, oxygen, and carbon
    C. Carbon, hydrogen, and oxygen
    D. Helium, hydrogen, and oxygen

15. The MINIMUM temperature for composting is

    A. 90° F
    B. 90° C
    C. 150° F
    D. 150° C

16. What is the permissible noise level for an 8-hour period according to the Occupational Safety and Health Administration? _____ dB.

    A. 100
    B. 90
    C. 80
    D. 70

17. Which of the following does NOT automatically constitute a recordable accident?

    A. First aid
    B. Broken bones
    C. Prescription medication
    D. Lost time from work

18. The Occupational Safety and Health Administration 200 log for recording accidents has to be filled out within _____ days after an accident.

    A. 3
    B. 5
    C. 20
    D. 60

19. If oil is spilled in a navigable waterway, the _____ must be notified.

    A. DEC
    B. Coast Guard
    C. Navy
    D. EPA

20. The two end products of combustion are

    A. CO_2 and H_2O
    B. CO_2 and CO
    C. H_2O and CO
    D. SO_2 and H_2O

21. Which of the following is a method of reducing NO_X emissions?

    A. Lower combustion fuel/air ratio
    B. Raise combustion fuel/air ratio
    C. Ammonia injection
    D. Increase yardwaste fuel percentage

22. The feedpump takes suction from the

    A. condenser
    B. deaerator
    C. steam drum
    D. condensate reservoir tanks

23. If you have three permits governing your operation - state, federal, and local - which limit do you have to meet?

    A. State
    B. Federal
    C. Local
    D. Most stringent

24. What is the box called that is found before the turbine inlet and after the turbine stop valves?

    A. Drain box
    B. Extraction chest
    C. Steam chest
    D. Stop chest

25. If garbage weighs 600 lb/cu.ft. and there is a landfill with 500,000 cu.ft. left in space, how much garbage, in tons, can be put into the landfill?

    A. 150,000
    B. 200,000
    C. 3,000,000
    D. 90,000,000

26. If you are conducting a speech at a media event and an irate person stands up and starts shouting at you, what should you do?

    A. Try to shout your speech over the top of his voice
    B. Point your finger at him and tell him to shut up and sit down
    C. Let him finish and then repeat his concerns
    D. Tell him that he will have to leave the room if he continues to act like a juvenile

27. What should be the O_2 content in combustion air?

    A. 19%   B. 8%   C. 30%   D. 21%

4 (#1)

28. The BEST method of cleaning the waterside of boiler tubes is by   28.____

    A. steam   B. chemical   C. heat   D. dry

29. Of the following flow-control devices, the MOST often used are   29.____

    A. weight loaded valves   B. orifices
    C. hydraulic valves   D. gate valves

30. What negative effect does chlorine in municipal solid waste have?   30.____

    A. Corrodes lower furnace of boilers
    B. Causes plugs in ESPs and fabric filters
    C. Increases lime consumption
    D. Decreases heat transfer in the economizer

31. 144,783 gallons would equal _____ cu.ft.   31.____

    A. 19,356   B. 22,678   C. 19,223   D. 20,344

32. I. Paper   40%   @7200 BTU/lb =   2880   32.____
         Glass   9%   @2300 BTU/lb =   207
         Petroleum   15%   @9600 BTU/lb =   1440
         Metal   23%   @1900 BTU/lb =   437
         Plastic   13%   @8400 BTU/lb =   1092
                     100%   6056 BTU/lb

     II. Paper   38%
         Glass   12%
         Petroleum   8%
         Metal   25%
         Plastic   17%
                     100%   ???? BTU/lb

    Given the above compositions of two 1-lb. garbage samples, what BTU/lb value does the second sample contain?
    A. 4978 BTU/lb   B. 5776 BTU/lb
    C. 5564 BTU/lb   D. 5683 BTU/lb

33. Incinerator ash is classified as _____ waste.   33.____

    A. toxic   B. safe
    C. special   D. radioactive

34. Which of the following is NOT normally monitored for emissions?   34.____

    A. HCl   B. SO_2 C. CO   D. Hg

35. 210 lb/hr steam flow would convert to _____ gallons/minute.   35.____

    A. .42   B. .84   C. 1.04   D. 1.77

KEY (CORRECT ANSWERS)

1.	C	16.	C
2.	B	17.	A
3.	D	18.	B
4.	A	19.	B
5.	B	20.	A
6.	A	21.	C
7.	C	22.	B
8.	B	23.	D
9.	D	24.	C
10.	A	25.	A
11.	D	26.	C
12.	B	27.	D
13.	A	28.	B
14.	C	29.	B
15.	A	30.	A

31. A
32. D
33. C
34. A
35. A

———

TEST 2

DIRECTIONS: Each question or incomplete statement is followed by several suggested answers or completions. Select the one that BEST answers the question or completes the statement. *PRINT THE LETTER OF THE CORRECT ANSWER IN THE SPACE AT THE RIGHT.*

1. What is the ideal moisture content for composting? 1.____

    A. 75%   B. 90%   C. 50%   D. 85%

2. The MAIN purpose of running open piping through landfills is to 2.____

    A. separate waste piles
    B. act as tunnels to discourage vermin
    C. collect leachate so it can be removed and treated
    D. inject chemicals into the waste

3. The MOST effective way to reduce acid gas production and emissions is to remove _____ from the waste stream. 3.____

    A. metal   B. batteries
    C. yard waste   D. wood and wood products

4. A resource recovery plant's power is measured in 4.____

    A. KW   B. watts   C. joules   D. MW

5. Steam in the presence of water is 5.____

    A. superheated   B. vapor   C. saturated   D. sensible

6. What would cause particulate carryover in municipal solid waste boilers? 6.____

    A. Excessive combustion air   B. Insufficient underfire air
    C. Low draft   D. Wet refuse

7. When _____ are increased on a boiler, the natural circulation is improved. 7.____

    A. height and operating pressure
    B. operating pressure and operating temperature
    C. operating temperature and height
    D. operating pressure and number of waterwall tubes

8. 150 ft/25 sec converts to _____ ft/min. 8.____

    A. 720   B. 9000   C. 10   D. 360

9. Generators producing power in their rotating shaft transport that power off the shaft by use of 9.____

    A. slip rings and brushes
    B. commutators
    C. a rotating power transporter coupling
    D. magnets

10. A vacuum is created by

    A. cold water in a condenser
    B. air ejectors
    C. condensing steam
    D. gland seals

11. What is the acronym for the law governing the transportation, landfilling, and composting of municipal solid waste?

    A. DEC B. RCRA C. EPA D. RICO

12. Which of the following is a type of air preheater?

    A. Recuperative   B. Convective
    C. Transformative   D. All of the above

13. For a boiler with 500,000 sq.ft. or more heating space, at least _____ safeties are required.

    A. one B. two C. three D. four

14. The MAIN purpose of a municipal solid waste transfer station is to

    A. consolidate collection zones for traffic control
    B. check trucks for mechanical problems
    C. provide an area to check for *bulkies*
    D. save money for the citizens of the township

15. When bringing down a turbine for maintenance, the turbine turning gear engages

    A. when the turbine slows down to less than 500 rpm
    B. at 200 rpm
    C. after the turbine stops
    D. when the turbine casing temperature has dropped to 312 degrees F.

16. The purpose of grounding brushes on a generator is to

    A. transport generated power to the transformers
    B. prevent over-excitation of the shaft
    C. provide a safe path for stray currents, which would otherwise restrict power production
    D. prevent backflow of electricity

17. A turbine thrust bearing

    A. limits radial movement
    B. reduces vibration of the shaft
    C. limits axial movement
    D. diverts steam to the low pressure part of the turbine

18. Heat is transferred through a boiler tube by

   A. conduction B. convection
   C. radiation D. discombobulation

19. Heat is transferred through the boiler gas passes by

   A. conduction B. convection
   C. radiation D. refraction

20. _____ LEAST affects composting.

   A. Moisture B. Temperature
   C. Microorganisms D. Sunlight

21. If a boiler has to be down for an extended period of time, it should NOT be wet-stored if

   A. there is a possibility of the ambient temperature's dropping below the freezing point
   B. the waterside of the tubes needs to be cleaned
   C. the downtime is going to be over a year
   D. there are other boilers operating in the vicinity

22. The FIRST to be called during a plant emergency is the

   A. police
   B. plant manager
   C. fire department
   D. depends upon the situation

23. The two predominant heavy metals found in bottom ash are

   A. lead and mercury B. cadmium and lead
   C. cadmium and mercury D. lead and aluminum

24. What is the predominant heavy metal found in flue gas?

   A. Lead B. Cadmium C. Mercury D. Aluminum

25. The purpose of putting a topsoil cap on a landfill at the end of each day is that it

   A. allows grass to grow between layers of refuse
   B. discourages vermin and helps reduce odors
   C. provides a surface for trucks to drive on the next day
   D. helps prevent rain from leaching through refuse

26. The purpose of gland seals on a turbine is to

   A. prevent ambient air from entering or escaping turbine
   B. increase efficiency of turbine
   C. help prevent thermal stress on turbine shaft
   D. all of the above

4 (#2)

Questions 27-30.

DIRECTIONS: Questions 27 through 30 are to be answered on the basis of the following facts.

After being down for a week for maintenance, a boiler is ready to be brought back on line. The boiler has been filled to the correct drum level and all valving is correctly lined up to commence firing.

27. Which of the following valves should be in the open position on the boiler? 27.____

    A. Boiler drum vent
    B. Continuous blowdown
    C. Chemical feed
    D. Feedwater regulator

28. Upon firing, the drum level will 28.____

    A. drop
    B. remain at its present level until steam outlet valve is opened
    C. rise
    D. drop until the furnace reaches 900° F

29. What determines the time period in which it will take the boiler to completely warm up and be at full refuse burning load once firing has begun? 29.____

    A. Manpower
    B. Boiler metal stress considerations
    C. Fuel availability
    D. Plant water balance

30. If, upon sending steam down the main steam line, water hammer occurs, it is apparent that the 30.____

    A. steam outlet line was not warmed up correctly
    B. attemperator control valves were left open
    C. pressure was insufficient for sending steam downline
    D. all of the above

KEY (CORRECT ANSWERS)

1.	B	16.	C
2.	C	17.	C
3.	B	18.	A
4.	D	19.	B
5.	C	20.	D
6.	A	21.	A
7.	C	22.	D
8.	D	23.	B
9.	A	24.	C
10.	C	25.	B
11.	B	26.	A
12.	A	27.	A
13.	B	28.	C
14.	A	29.	B
15.	C	30.	A

EXAMINATION SECTION
TEST 1

DIRECTIONS: Each question or incomplete statement is followed by several suggested answers or completions. Select the one that BEST answers the question or completes the statement. *PRINT THE LETTER OF THE CORRECT ANSWER IN THE SPACE AT THE RIGHT.*

1. Which of the following is NOT included in the *ultimate analysis*? 1._____
   A. Carbon
   B. Sulfur
   C. Volatile matter
   D. Moisture

2. Which of the following is a component material in municipal solid waste? 2._____
   A. Fixed carbon
   B. Sulfur
   C. Rubber
   D. Hydrogen

3. Which of the following is an inorganic material? 3._____
   A. Paper
   B. Silica
   C. Wood
   D. Plastic

4. _____ wastes are excluded by the New Source Performance Standards' definition of municipal solid waste? 4._____
   A. Hazardous
   B. Batteries, tires, and used motor oil
   C. Household
   D. Commercial

5. The nitrogen oxide emissions from municipal waste collection units tends to peak in the summer on Mondays because 5._____
   A. parties occur on the weekends
   B. it rains on the weekends
   C. of increased weekend commercial activity
   D. of weekend yard wastes

6. Until the recent initiatives for recycling, the average individual in affluent communities produced _____ municipal solid waste as/than those in economically depressed areas. 6._____
   A. about the same
   B. more
   C. less
   D. there is no correlation

7. Monofills, in comparison with regulated hazardous waste landfills, 7._____
   A. can receive more types of waste materials
   B. can receive only one type of waste material
   C. have less exacting design and monitoring requirements
   D. have more exacting design and monitoring requirements

8. A _____ system does not meet the design requirements of monofills under current Resource Conservation and Recovery Act regulations.

    A. single liner
    B. leachate collection
    C. leachate monitoring
    D. methane gas monitoring

9. The yard clippings included in the municipal solid waste charged into municipal waste collections contribute to

    A. good burning conditions
    B. nitrogen oxide emissions
    C. a decrease in the fuel moisture
    D. all of the above

10. Operators must meet all of the following requirements EXCEPT be

    A. qualified and certified
    B. a certified emergency medical technician
    C. able to understand basic chemistry
    D. able to motivate workers

11. In the _____, the United States Congress instructed the Environmental Protection Agency to set standards for sanitary landfills.

    A. Standards of Performance for New Stationary Sources, municipal waste collections
    B. Comprehensive Environmental Response Compensation and Liability Act
    C. Clean Air Act Amendments of 1990
    D. Resource Conservation and Recovery Act of 1984

12. The environmental guidelines for existing municipal waste collection units does NOT require regulation of

    A. carbon monoxide
    B. nitric oxides
    C. sulfur oxides
    D. hydrogen chloride

13. Often considered to be undesirable or untreatable at municipal waste collection facilities are

    A. batteries
    B. scrap metal
    C. segregated medical wastes
    D. all of the above

14. It is NOT a function of the weigh scale operations to

    A. determine the amount of expense to charge each truck
    B. determine the amount of material received each day
    C. redirect inappropriate loads of waste materials to other facilities
    D. determine the carbon and metals composition in the ash leaving the unit

15. Generally considered to be the disposal technique of last resort is

    A. incineration
    B. recycling
    C. landfill
    D. source reduction

3 (#1)

16. _____ can lower disposal costs but often requires consumer products to be of higher quality with higher manufacturing costs.

    A. Incineration
    B. Recycling
    C. Landfill
    D. Source reduction

17. The process of recycling programs which does NOT improve the combustion quality of municipal solid waste charged into a mass burn municipal waste collection is

    A. composting
    B. metal removal
    C. glass removal
    D. paper removal

18. A general refuse derived fuel program can _____ the heating value of the municipal solid waste entering the combustion unit.

    A. *increase* by 10%
    B. *decrease* by 10%
    C. *increase* by 25%
    D. *decrease* by 25%

19. An average higher heating value of the conventional refuse derived fuel is APPROXIMATELY _____ BTU/lbm.

    A. 2,000   B. 4,000   C. 6,000   D. 8,000

20. The ash fusion temperature of municipal solid waste varies from about 1300° F to _____ ° F, compared with 2100 to 2500° F for bituminous coal.

    A. 1600   B. 2100   C. 2500   D. 6000

21. The PRIMARY activity of a _____ is to break open plastic bags of municipal solid waste.

    A. Trommel screen
    B. shredder
    C. flail mill
    D. air classifier

22. The PRIMARY activity of a _____ is to segregate the metal and grit pieces from the larger pieces.

    A. Trommel screen
    B. magnetic separator
    C. flail mill
    D. air classifier

23. A population of 100,000 people on average produces about _____ municipal solid waste per day.

    A. 350 tons
    B. 1,000 lbm.
    C. 350,000 lbm.
    D. 3,500,000 lbm.

24. The APPROXIMATE amount of air, in pounds, required to burn a pound of dry paper is

    A. 0.5   B. 3   C. 6   D. 12

25. The APPROXIMATE amount of air, in pounds, required to burn a pound of dry paper at around 100% excess air is

    A. 0.5   B. 3   C. 6   D. 12

KEY (CORRECT ANSWERS)

1.	C	11.	D
2.	C	12.	B
3.	B	13.	D
4.	A	14.	D
5.	D	15.	C
6.	B	16.	D
7.	B	17.	D
8.	A	18.	C
9.	B	19.	C
10.	B	20.	A

21. C
22. A
23. C
24. C
25. D

TEST 2

DIRECTIONS: Each question or incomplete statement is followed by several suggested answers or completions. Select the one that BEST answers the question or completes the statement. *PRINT THE LETTER OF THE CORRECT ANSWER IN THE SPACE AT THE RIGHT.*

1. Silicon carbide coatings are generally placed on the waterwall surfaces below the over-fire air ports to

    A. reflect the combustion energy and keep the waterwalls from overheating
    B. prevent sequential oxidation and reduction reactions on the metal walls
    C. eliminate carbon monoxide formation
    D. reduce the costs of water treatment

    1.____

2. A properly operating in situ monitor indicates 300 ppm of SO_2 in the flue gas, with the moisture in the flue gas known to be 20%.
If an extractive instrument which has an in-line dryer indicates 320 ppm of SO_2, then the

    A. two instruments are reading consistently
    B. extractive instrument is reading too high
    C. extractive instrument is reading too low
    D. two instruments are reading erratically

    2.____

3. Properly operating extractive instruments indicate 200 ppm of SO_2 and 9% oxygen in the flue gas.
The standard emission concentration of SO_2 corrected to 7% flue gas oxygen would be _____ ppm of SO_2

    A. 200   B. 233   C. 171   D. 333

    3.____

4. The overall amount of excess air used in modular, starved-air incinerators is about _____ that of conventional grate firing, mass burn systems.

    A. half   B. twice   C. ten times   D. the same as

    4.____

5. Volatile metals tend to be concentrated on sub-micron particulate matter in the exhaust. This phenomena occurs because

    A. those metals are contained on small diameter particulates in the waste fuel
    B. upon being heated in the furnace, they swell up and burst into lots of fine particles
    C. after being vaporized in the furnace, they are subsequently condensed onto the surface of particulate matter, which is mostly associated with small diameter particulates
    D. air pollution control devices have high efficiencies for capture of the large particulates

    5.____

6. Nitrogen oxides formed from molecular nitrogen in air is referred to as *thermal NOx* because

    A. nitrogen oxide burns the skin
    B. its formation has a negative impact on the thermal efficiency of the boiler
    C. the formation reaction rate is greatly increased with increasing temperature
    D. when it is formed the combustion gas will begin to glow brightly

    6.____

7. By injecting ammonia or urea into the furnace, reactions are established which will convert NOx into molecular reactions.
   These reactions occur at about _____ °F.

   A. 2100-2300   B. 1600-1800   C. 1200-1400   D. 800-1000

8. A potential problem with ammonia or urea injection for NOx control is the formation of a white plume.
   This is caused by

   A. steam in the flue gas condensing more rapidly
   B. formation of ammonium chloride which condenses as a white particulate in the plume
   C. urea and ammonia being injected into the system as white materials
   D. ammonium sulfate being formed in the flue gases

9. In any combustion system, a portion of the inorganic material in the flue will be released as fly ash. For a pulverized coal-fired utility boiler, about 80% of the ash leaves the boiler as fly ash.
   The amount of the fuel ash which leaves a conventional mass burn, water wall facility as fly ash is APPROXIMATELY _____ %.

   A. 40-60   B. 20-40   C. 10-20   D. 1-10

10. Why do mass burn excess-air units use pusher grates?

    A. Pieces of mass burn materials clump together and are too large to get good carbon burnout on a travelling grate.
    B. A larger fraction of the mass burn materials burn in suspension, which causes higher bed temperatures which would destroy travelling grates.
    C. Mass burn units have more glass and aluminum which would melt and produce a lot more clinkers if it were burned on a travelling grate.
    D. None of the above

11. On average, the combustion gases leaving the burning region of the fuel bed in an excess-air waterwall unit will GENERALLY be

    A. fuel-rich (starved-air conditions)
    B. at approximately stoichiometric conditions
    C. fuel-lean (excess air conditions)
    D. none of the above

12. Using the regulatory definition, the combustion efficiency of a modern, waterwall municipal waste collection unit *based on the flue gas carbon monoxide to carbon dioxide ratio is* _____ %

    A. 25-40   B. 70-85
    C. 85-97   D. greater than 99

13. The overall energy conversion efficiency of a modern, waterwall municipal waste collection unit based on fuel energy to electrical energy production is _____ %.

    A. 25-40   B. 70-85
    C. 85-95   D. greater than 95

14. During start-up, auxiliary fuel burners are used to preheat the boiler. The operator is required to assure that the

     A. waste will light off properly without excess smoking
     B. furnace temperature is high enough to assure burnout of organics and CO coming from the fuel bed
     C. grate bars are at the proper temperature level prior to waste charging
     D. solid deposits have been burned off the boiler walls

14._____

15. Initiation of air preheating during normal operations of a mass burn municipal waste collection is an operator decision PRIMARILY based on

     A. a need for more steam production
     B. the general moisture content of the waste
     C. control of the air pollution control device inlet temperature
     D. the amount of plastic material in the waste fuel

15._____

16. Which of the following characteristics are typical for a deaerator?

     A. 50 to 100 psig operating pressure
     B. Preheating condensate to saturation at 5 to 10 psig pressure
     C. Cooling the condensate to less than 212° F
     D. Superheating condensate but at a slight vacuum

16._____

17. The feedwater pumps in a municipal waste collection steam system are designed to

     A. raise the feedwater pressure to about 65% of the boiler design pressure
     B. raise the feedwater pressure to the full boiler operating pressure
     C. recirculate water from the turbine to the condensate hot well prior to entering the economizer
     D. circulate water in a loop between the condenser and , cooling tower

17._____

18. The turbine generator rotational speed must be slowly increased from the turning gear rate to synchronization speed to

     A. make certain that the turning gear disengages at the right time
     B. assure that the rotational speed never exceeds 3600 rpm
     C. allow for expansion of the rotor and casing
     D. provide a smooth transition from single phase to three phase power production

18._____

19. In situ instruments for measuring flue gas concentrations have typical features which

     A. allow them to give readings which are identical with those of extractive monitoring instruments
     B. provide concentration readings which are higher than extractive instruments due to the influence of water vapor
     C. are more reliable than extractive systems because of their high temperature exposures
     D. allow for monitoring the gas under its actual stack conditions

19._____

20. The MOST difficult operational problem for measuring flue gas concentrations that is associated with in situ instruments is

    A. obtaining a dry gas sample before it is analyzed
    B. keeping the gas at the stack temperature to prevent chemical reactions
    C. providing for calibration
    D. keeping the unit operating appropriately in its harsh environment

21. A modern municipal waste collection facility was equipped with both *in situ* and *extractive* monitors for CO, and a moisture analyzer. The in situ monitors indicated 64 ppm CO, while the extractive monitor indicated 75 ppm CO.
    The moisture analyzer reading was 15%.
    In this situation,

    A. the in situ monitor reading was too low
    B. the extractive system was reading too high
    C. both instruments were reading correctly
    D. there was an air leak in the extractive system sampling line

22. Chemiluminescent NOx monitors must be routinely calibrated with both a span gas and a zero gas.
    The need for a zero gas calibration is that

    A. the photomultiplier tube, which produces an electrical signal (dark current) even when no gas is flowing through the detection cell, must have a method to calibrate the zero condition
    B. clean dry gas helps to clean out the capillaries within the instrument
    C. the measurement technique is based on the ratio of oxygen to nitrogen in standard air
    D. the zero gas serves as an internal standard for correcting the measurement to a desired percentage of oxygen

23. Which of the following chemical structures describes the 2,3,7,8 tetrachlorinated dibenzo-p-dioxin?

    A. [structure]
    B. [structure]
    C. [structure]
    D. [structure]

24. The MOST toxic of all polychlorinated dibenzo-p-dioxins is 24._____

    A. 2, 3, 7, 8 tetrachlorinated dibenzo-p-dioxin
    B. penta chlorodibenzo-p-dioxin
    C. octa chlorodibenzo-p-dioxin
    D. mono chlorodibenzo-p-dioxin

25. The required annual sampling procedures for measuring particulate mass emissions and 25._____
    dioxin/furan emissions both rely on a form of measurement based on a modification of
    the standard Environmental Protection Agency Method

    A. AP42   B. 5   C. 12   D. 111(b)

KEY (CORRECT ANSWERS)

1. B	11. A
2. C	12. D
3. B	13. A
4. D	14. B
5. C	15. B
6. C	16. B
7. B	17. B
8. B	18. C
9. D	19. D
10. A	20. D

21. C
22. A
23. C
24. A
25. B

EXAMINATION SECTION
TEST 1

DIRECTIONS: Each question or incomplete statement is followed by several suggested answers or completions. Select the one that BEST answers the question or completes the statement. *PRINT THE LETTER OF THE CORRECT ANSWER IN THE SPACE AT THE RIGHT.*

Questions 1-3.

DIRECTIONS: Questions 1 through 3 are to be answered on the basis of the following information.

A boiler has been off line for five days for maintenance and you are now ready to put it back into service. As you complete your walk down procedures, you check everything out and you have a normal operating level of water.

1. In what order do you start your fans?

   A. FD, ID, then OF   B. ID, OF, then FD
   C. ID, FD, then OF   D. OF, ID, then FD

2. You should run your fans for five minutes before lighting a fire in order to

   A. make sure fans are in proper operating condition
   B. cool refractory down to room temperature
   C. purge any possible combustible gas out of the furnace
   D. cool the steam drum down

3. What should you do when your water level swells due to warm-up heat?

   A. Shut off fuel, kill the fans, and add feedwater
   B. Leave fuel and fans on and add feedwater
   C. Screw down non-return valve
   D. Open blow-down valves

4. The reason the water level rises in a boiler during startup is that the

   A. feedwater valve is in automatic mode
   B. warm-up heat causes the steam drum to contract
   C. warm-up heat causes water to expand
   D. continuous blowdown is not functioning

5. A boiler is on line making steam, your CO monitor is reading 50 ppm, and the garbage is wet. All of a sudden, your CO reading jumps to 600 ppm, and your indicator lights indicate that all fan motors are running. Position indicators indicate that all fan dampers are correctly positioned and your air flow indicator indicates zero air flow.
What is the FIRST thing you should check?

   A. Damper linkage
   B. Fan drive belts
   C. The gate on the charging hopper
   D. Steam flow to the air preheater

6. You are firing RDF in an RDF furnace on RDF grates. An efficiency graph for your boiler indicates that with an increase in primary air temperature, your combustion efficiency is improved.
   When you can look at this chart and determine that it is more efficient to operate at 600°, why do you choose 400° temperature for primary air?

   A. The required air preheater would take up too much floor space.
   B. It would take too long to preheat the combustion air to the higher temperature.
   C. The required stack height would be excessive at 600°.
   D. The grate temperatures would be excessive at 600°.

7. If you notice your grate temperature is high, you should

   A. reduce the steam to the air preheater steam coils
   B. decrease the amount of underfire air
   C. increase the amount of fuel on grates
   D. shut fuel off to the boiler

8. _____ will pass through a demineralizer system unchanged.

   A. Silica   B. Oxygen   C. Chlorine   D. Nitrogen

9. When a silica meter reads high on a demineralizer system, it indicates that

   A. you need more acid in the resin beads
   B. your cation unit needs to be regenerated
   C. your anion unit needs to be regenerated
   D. you need more caustic in the cation unit

10. What is the drain line called at the approximate normal water level of the steam drum?

    A. Bottom blow   B. Skimmer
    C. Feedwater regulator   D. Boiler drain

11. If a steam drum is located 100 feet above sea level and the gauge reads 650 lbs. psig, what is the absolute pressure, in psia?

    A. 635.3   B. 664.7   C. 709.3   D. 1229.6

12. When heat is transferred from the boiler tube to the water in the tube, it is accomplished by _____ heat transfer.

    A. radiant   B. conduction
    C. convection   D. thermal

13. The _____ valve is ahead of the turbine throttle valve.

    A. governor   B. recirculation
    C. stop   D. gland seal

14. The stop valve

    A. controls the steam flow
    B. stops the steam in emergency situations
    C. drains the steam line
    D. controls back pressure

15. The large area between the stop valve and the throttle valve is called the   15.____

    A. expansion chamber   B. steam chest
    C. cylinder   D. exhaust chamber

16. The thrust bearing in a steam turbine acts against _____ force.   16.____

    A. radial   B. axial   C. lateral   D. vertical

17. If a landfill life is 500,000 cubic yards and the compacted density is 600 lbs. per cubic   17.____
    yard, how many tons would there be in the remaining life of the landfill?

    A. 125,000   B. 150,000   C. 175,000   D. 300,000

18. What is the periodic symbol for lead?   18.____

    A. Pb   B. Cd   C. Le   D. Ld

19. What is the chemical symbol for cadmium?   19.____

    A. Pb   B. Cd   C. Cm   D. Ci

20. The MOST effective composting occurs between _____ °F.   20.____

    A. 55 to 130   B. 130 to 160
    C. 165 to 180   D. 185 to 210

21. What has the HIGHEST concentration of sulfur in the waste stream?   21.____

    A. Gypsum board   B. Batteries
    C. Paper   D. Plastics

22. What impact do batteries have on acid emissions?   22.____

    A. Large increase in sulfur dioxides
    B. Small increase in nitrous oxides
    C. Negligible increase in hydrochloric acid
    D. None

23. When using a negative pressure respirator with standard cartridges, what are you pro-   23.____
    tecting employees against?

    A. Inert gases laden with dust
    B. Small particles of dust and mist
    C. Flue gases
    D. Oxygen deficiency

24. You can maintain an efficient vacuum in a condenser by using   24.____

    A. a large vacuum pump
    B. cold circulating water
    C. steam jet air ejectors
    D. condensate pumps

25. What is the LARGEST concentration of ferrous in a municipal solid waste stream made up of? 25._____

   A. Sheet metal
   B. Soda and beer cans
   C. Food cans
   D. Appliances

KEY (CORRECT ANSWERS)

1. C
2. C
3. D
4. C
5. B

6. D
7. A
8. C
9. C
10. B

11. B
12. C
13. C
14. B
15. B

16. B
17. B
18. A
19. B
20. B

21. A
22. D
23. B
24. B
25. C

TEST 2

DIRECTIONS: Each question or incomplete statement is followed by several suggested answers or completions. Select the one that BEST answers the question or completes the statement. *PRINT THE LETTER OF THE CORRECT ANSWER IN THE SPACE AT THE RIGHT.*

1. According to the OSHA 200 Log, an injury must be recorded within _____ days after it occurs.

    A. two B. six C. ten D. thirty

2. An injury does NOT have to be reported when _____ was required.

    A. light duty
    B. only first aid
    C. medical treatment
    D. time off the job

3. If you are running a generator not synchronized with a major network, you can control the frequency by using a _____ control.

    A. excitation voltage
    B. master steam
    C. speed
    D. steam pressure

4. The MAIN purpose of a condensate pump is to

    A. provide cooling water to the condenser
    B. move water out of the hot well
    C. feed the boiler feedwater pump
    D. move water to the hot well

5. An integral part of a condenser is a

    A. condensate pump
    B. steam jet air ejector
    C. vacuum pump
    D. hot well

6. A feedwater pump gets its water from the

    A. hot well
    B. condensate pumps
    C. low pressure heater
    D. DA storage tank

7. The pressure in a boiler is maintained by the

    A. rate of firing
    B. feedpumps
    C. steam header pressure
    D. steam flow

8. A boiler is evaporating 60,000 lbs. of water per hour, burning 10 tons of RDF with a heat content of 4,500 BTU/lb. What would the BTU content, in BTU/lb., be at 50,000 lbs. of water per hour, burning 10 tons of RDF?

    A. 4,375 B. 5,625 C. 3,750 D. 3,575

9. _____ ash is the WORST source of fugitive dust in a power plant.

    A. Fly
    B. Bottom
    C. Siftings
    D. Reinjection

10. If an incident occurs at your plant that causes public concern, the BEST way to conduct yourself in dealing with the news media is to

A. tell the news media and the public that the incident is too technical for them to understand
B. avoid the news media completely
C. be honest with your answers and let the news media know that you are concerned about your operation and its impact on the public health and safety, and if there is something that you do not have an answer for, you will find out and get back to them
D. make up something to tell the news media and the public that does not seem quite as serious to them

11. If a pressure gauge reads 125 psi at the pump discharge, how high can the water be lifted?
    _____ ft.
    A. 125   B. 215   C. 250   D. 289

12. A pump delivers 300,000 gallons of water per hour to a height of 250 feet. If the pump is 65% efficient, what horsepower is required to deliver this water?
    A. 320   B. 485   C. 4,548   D. 18,939

13. How many gallons of water are there in one cubic foot?
    A. 7.48   B. 7.50   C. 8.339   D. 62.34

14. How much does a cubic foot of water weigh, in lbs.?
    A. 7.480   B. 8.339   C. 62.4   D. 433.0

15. The common term for securing a piece of equipment for maintenance is
    A. power down   B. off line
    C. tag out   D. disconnect

16. If a pump pumped 250,170 pounds of water in one hour, how many gallons per minute would that be?
    A. 555.9   B. 502.4   C. 500.0   D. 497.6

17. If a boiler had 500 square feet of heating surface, how many safety valves would be required?
    A. 4   B. 3   C. 2   D. 1

18. How many cubic inches are there in one cubic foot?
    A. .0361   B. 144   C. 231   D. 1,728

19. If you have water and steam in the same line, the temperature would be
    A. 100° C   B. 212° F
    C. saturated   D. superheated

20. At 2 psia, the saturation temperature is _____ ° F.
    A. 126.08   B. 101.74   C. 218.11   D. 227.96

21. At standard atmospheric pressure, the saturation temperature is

    A. 101.74 B. 193.21 C. 212.00 D. 213.03

22. If your flue gas temperature is high, it could be caused by

    A. low excess air
    B. high excess air
    C. fire side tube fouling
    D. low boiler water level

23. If the water side of the pressure vessel is scaled up, what is the prescribed method of cleaning?

    A. Blasting
    B. Chemical
    C. Deslagging
    D. Increase boiler water temperature

24. When laying up a boiler with pendent type superheater tubes, you would NOT want them full of water when the

    A. boiler outlet valve is being worked on
    B. boiler penthouse is being cleaned
    C. temperature is low enough that they might freeze
    D. boiler water storage tank has a low level

25. What are some of the hazards of operating a boiler with a high water level?

    A. Increased expense for treated water
    B. Possibility of water washing the turbine blades
    C. Loss of boiler efficiency
    D. All of the above

KEY (CORRECT ANSWERS)

1. B		11. D	
2. B		12. B	
3. C		13. A	
4. B		14. C	
5. D		15. C	
6. D		16. C	
7. A		17. D	
8. C		18. D	
9. A		19. C	
10. C		20. A	

21. C
22. C
23. B
24. C
25. B

EXAMINATION SECTION
TEST 1

DIRECTIONS: Each question or incomplete statement is followed by several suggested answers or completions. Select the one that BEST answers the question or completes the statement. *PRINT THE LETTER OF THE CORRECT ANSWER IN THE SPACE AT THE RIGHT.*

1. The MOST efficient devices to measure the gaseous pollutant content of an air sample are

    A. cyclones
    B. filters
    C. bubblers
    D. settling chambers

    1._____

2. The source MOST likely to cause high concentrations of toxic metals associated with nonpoint source water pollution is

    A. construction
    B. highway de-icing
    C. on-site sewage disposal
    D. urban storm runoff

    2._____

3. In the United States, the required landfill space per person each year is GENERALLY

    A. ten cubic feet
    B. one cubic yard
    C. one cubic acre
    D. ten square feet

    3._____

4. The easiest and most effective method for controlling air pollution is

    A. source correction
    B. treatment
    C. collection
    D. dispersion

    4._____

5. The MOST serious source of air pollution associated with the automobile is the

    A. fuel tank
    B. carburetor
    C. crankcase
    D. exhaust

    5._____

6. Which of the following practices or devices is considered to be a collection or treatment control for urban storm-water runoff?

    A. Anti-littering laws
    B. Street cleaning
    C. Floodplain zoning
    D. Detention systems

    6._____

7. The increasing trend in solid waste disposal in the United States is toward the practice of

    A. incineration
    B. ocean dumping
    C. sanitary landfill
    D. recycling/resource reclamation

    7._____

8. The MOST widely practiced method for cooling air pollutants before they reach control equipment is

    A. dilution
    B. settling
    C. heat exchange coils
    D. quenching

    8._____

9. Which of the following is NOT a factor of required knowledge for solving an upgrade problem in wastewater treatment plants?

    9._____

47

A. Staffing pattern
B. Normal operational and maintenance procedures
C. Daily peak flow rates
D. Condition of process hardware

10. The category of solid waste that constitutes the GREATEST volume percentage in the United States is

    A. residential
    B. bulky wastes
    C. commercial
    D. industrial

11. In current practice, the SIMPLEST test for ozone content of an air sample measures the air's reaction with

    A. metals with high lead content
    B. rubber
    C. organics
    D. copper

12. High concentrations of acid pollutants associated with nonpoint source water pollution are MOST likely to be contributed by

    A. non-coal mining
    B. air pollution fallout
    C. agriculture
    D. forestry

13. Which of the following methods is used by analysts to measure the concentration of hydrocarbons in an air supply?

    A. Chemical luminescence
    B. Flame ionization
    C. Infrared spectrometry
    D. High-volume sampling

14. Environmental engineers generally consider _____ to be the BEST cover material for sanitary landfill sites.

    A. sandy loam
    B. clay
    C. gravel
    D. silt

15. Deceleration of an automobile is most likely to cause the HIGHEST relative increase in the amount of

    A. hydrocarbons
    B. carbon monoxide
    C. nitrogen oxides
    D. lead

16. The _____ method for sanitary landfilling involves the distribution of waste into discrete *cells*.

    A. slope   B. area   C. ramp   D. trench

17. A DISADVANTAGE associated with the use of controlled burning for solid waste disposal is

    A. consumption of a large amount of resources
    B. lingering contamination of burn site
    C. increased transport costs
    D. large land area required

18. Each of the following is a primary factor in the determination of the area required for a sanitary landfill site EXCEPT

    A. percent reduction, by compaction, of on-site refuse volume
    B. amount of cover material required
    C. total projected amount of refuse to be delivered
    D. average density of refuse delivered to landfill

    18.____

19. The method of solid waste disposal that currently involves the GREATEST costs in capital investment is

    A. incineration
    B. ocean dumping
    C. landfilling
    D. composting

    19.____

20. The substance normally used in filters to detect the presence of sulfur dioxide in an air sample is

    A. microorganisms
    B. sulfur
    C. lead peroxide
    D. carbon

    20.____

21. Which of the following is NOT a quality parameter of concern in the activated carbon treatment of wastewater?

    A. Heavy metals
    B. Suspended solids
    C. Trace organics
    D. Dissolved oxygen

    21.____

22. The problem that presents the GREATEST potential hazard to landfill sites is

    A. pests
    B. water pollution
    C. gas
    D. decomposition

    22.____

23. The MOST serious problem associated with the investigative practice of industrial stack sampling is

    A. control of potentially great capital expense
    B. risk of obtaining an unrepresentative sample
    C. safety risks for analysts
    D. skewing of sample readings by heat concentrations

    23.____

24. The MOST common method for disinfection in wastewater treatment plants is

    A. ozone treatment
    B. ultraviolet light exposure
    C. chlorination
    D. introduction of bromine chloride

    24.____

25. Of the following categories for the pollution control of urban stormwater runoff, _____ controls are considered to be the MOST effective and inexpensive.

    A. planning
    B. accumulation
    C. treatment
    D. collection

    25.____

KEY (CORRECT ANSWERS)

1. C
2. D
3. B
4. A
5. D

6. D
7. D
8. C
9. C
10. D

11. B
12. A
13. B
14. A
15. A

16. B
17. C
18. C
19. D
20. C

21. A
22. B
23. B
24. C
25. A

TEST 2

DIRECTIONS: Each question or incomplete statement is followed by several suggested answers or completions. Select the one that BEST answers the question or completes the statement. *PRINT THE LETTER OF THE CORRECT ANSWER IN THE SPACE AT THE RIGHT.*

1. _____% of solid waste in the United States is considered compostible.
   A. 5-10 B. 20-30 C. 50-75 D. 80-85

2. Which of the following is NOT considered to be a factor affecting the level of organic decomposition in sanitary landfills?
   A. Moisture
   B. Surface area of fill
   C. Temperature
   D. Depth of fill

3. The SIMPLEST and MOST widely used device for controlling the particulate content of an air supply is the
   A. settling chamber
   B. adsorber
   C. wet collector
   D. bubbler

4. The agricultural practice MOST likely to contribute high levels of total dissolved solids to nonpoint source water pollution is
   A. animal production
   B. irrigated crop production
   C. pasturing and rangeland
   D. non-irrigated crop production

5. Pathogenic bacteria in wastewater supplies are likely to be produced by each of the following EXCEPT
   A. construction operations
   B. food processing industries
   C. pharmaceutical manufacturing
   D. tanneries

6. The substance MOST often used to remove sulfur from discharged flue gases is
   A. copper B. lime C. water D. acid

7. In controlling automotive emissions, an activated carbon canister is used to store emissions from the
   A. manifold
   B. fuel tank
   C. crankcase
   D. exhaust

8. Which of the following is NOT a disadvantage associated with the use of sanitary landfill sites for solid waste disposal?
   A. High collection costs
   B. Jurisdiction entanglements
   C. Large amount of land required
   D. Difficulties presented by seasonal changes

9. The Ringelmann scale is a device used to measure the _____ of an air sample. 9.____

   A. smoke density B. odor
   C. temperature D. gaseous pollutant content

10. High-volume sampling is a method for detecting 10.____

    A. ozone B. oxidant
    C. particulate D. sulfur dioxide

11. An example of air pollution abatement, as opposed to source control, is 11.____

    A. change of raw material B. modification of process
    C. equipment modifications D. stack dispersion

12. *Pollutant loading* is a term that defines the 12.____

    A. collection of pollutants for treatment in a control exercise
    B. quantity of pollution detached and transported into surface watercourses
    C. saturation point of any environment in terms of its pollutant capacity
    D. process of contamination, by an industrial source, of the ambient air

13. Each of the following is an advantage associated with the controlled burning of solid wastes EXCEPT 13.____

    A. land can be returned to immediate use
    B. sites are longer-lasting
    C. reduced amount of required land
    D. relatively easy collection and transport of materials

14. The device capable of removing the smallest particle from an air supply is the 14.____

    A. electrostatic precipitator
    B. settling chamber
    C. bag filter
    D. wet collector

15. High concentrations of suspended solids associated with nonpoint source water pollution are MOST likely contributed by 15.____

    A. urban storm runoff
    B. construction
    C. air pollution fallout
    D. non-irrigated crop production

16. Which of the following is NOT one of the primary steps involved in the control of gaseous air pollutants? 16.____

    A. Removal of pollutant from emissions
    B. Change in process producing pollutant
    C. Dispersion of the pollutant
    D. Chemical conversion of the pollutant

17. To control automotive air pollution, the process of recycling blow-by gases is a method for controlling emissions from the

    A. fuel tank
    B. exhaust
    C. carburetor
    D. crankcase

    17.____

18. In testing a water supply for the presence of coliform bacteria, the survey method MOST likely to be used is

    A. oxygen demand
    B. dissolved oxygen
    C. total dissolved solids
    D. suspended solids

    18.____

19. In measuring the constituency of a given air supply, analysts use the process of infrared spectrometry to determine concentrations of

    A. oxidants
    B. carbon monoxide
    C. sulfur dioxide
    D. particulates

    19.____

20. Which of the following is NOT one of the primary factors affecting the choice of pollution control methods for urban stormwater runoff?

    A. Specific constituents of runoff
    B. Type of sewage system
    C. Status of area development
    D. Method of land use

    20.____

21. A disadvantage associated with the use of sanitary landfill sites for solid waste disposal is

    A. high personnel and plant costs
    B. weakened accomodation of peak quantities
    C. potential for groundwater pollution
    D. difficulty with unusual, bulky materials

    21.____

22. The MOST serious problem in air pollution is presented by

    A. cooling of pollutants
    B. treatment of pollutants
    C. collection of pollutants
    D. source modifications

    22.____

23. Of the following practices or devices, the one considered to be an accumulation control for urban stormwater runoff is

    A. automobile inspection
    B. street cleaning
    C. floodplain zoning
    D. catch basins

    23.____

24. _____ is used to survey an air sample for the presence of sulfur dioxide.

    A. Liquid medium
    B. Colorimetry
    C. High-volume sampling
    D. Flame ionization

    24.____

25. Acceleration of an automobile is most likely to cause the HIGHEST relative increase in the amount of

    A. hydrocarbons
    B. carbon monoxide
    C. nitrogen oxides
    D. lead

    25.____

KEY (CORRECT ANSWERS)

1. D
2. B
3. A
4. B
5. A

6. B
7. B
8. A
9. A
10. C

11. D
12. B
13. D
14. A
15. B

16. C
17. D
18. A
19. B
20. A

21. C
22. C
23. B
24. B
25. C

EXAMINATION SECTION
TEST 1

DIRECTIONS: Each question or incomplete statement is followed by several suggested answers or completions. Select the one that BEST answers the question or competes the statement. *PRINT THE LETTER OF THE CORRECT ANSWER IN THE SPACE AT THE RIGHT.*

1. A MAJOR cause of air pollution resulting from the burning of fuel oils is _____ dioxide. 1.____
   A. sulfur   B. silicon   C. nitrous   D. hydrogen

2. Which one of the following components of fuel oil is limited by law to reduce air pollution? 2.____
   A. Carbon   B. Nitrogen   C. Hydrogen   D. Sulfur

3. Which of the following statements is INCORRECT? 3.____
   A. An air contaminant which is as dark or derker than #1 (on chart) but lighter then #2 shall not be emitted in any 1 hour for an aggregated period of 2 minutes.
   B. An air contaminant which is as dark or darker than #2 (on chart) but lighter than #3 shall not be enitted in any 1 hour for an aggregated period of 2 minutes.
   C. No air contaminant shall be emitted which is as dark or darker than #3 (on chart).
   D. On a six Ringelmann chart, #0, 1, 2, 3, 4, 5 is used to measure smoke density.

4. The sulfur content by weight of solid fuel on a dry basis or residual fuel oil burned in the city shall NOT exceed 4.____
   A. 1.1%   B. 2.2%   C. 3.3%   D. 4.4%

5. The one of the following coals that can LEGALLY be burned in city power plants is 5.____
   A. anthracite   B. sub-bituminous
   C. non-coking   D. bituminous

6. No air contaminant (smoke) shall be emitted which is as darker or darer than number 6.____
   A. 1   B. 2   C. 4   D. 5

7. An air contaminant (smoke) as dark or darker than No. 1 on the standard Ringelmann smoke chart but less than No. 2 shall NOT be emitted in any one hour for an aggregate period in excess of _____ minute(s). 7.____
   A. 1   B. 2   C. 3   D. 4

8. On the standard Ringelmann smoke chart, a No. 3 density indicates _____% black smoke. 8.____
   A. 3   B. 30   C. 60   D. 100

9. On a hand-fired boiler, what is the HIGHEST allowable amount of volatile matter in the coal expressed on an ash-free, moisture-free basis? 9.____
   A. 8%   B. 14%   C. 20%   D. 26%

10. On a stoker fired boiler which does not have a combustion controller, the HIGHEST allowable amount of volatile matter in the coal expressed on an ash-free, moisture-free basis is _____%.

    A. 10 B. 20 C. 30 D. 40

11. The total heat, in fuel, burned by a boiler running at maximum capacity is 10 million BTU per hour; in other words, its capacity rating is 10 million BTU input per hour.
    Under the Code, the MAXIMUM allowable emission of particulate matter (dust) for each million BTU per hour input is _____ lbs.

    A. 0.90 B. 0.75 C. 0.60 D. 0.18

12. The MAXIMUM allowable sulfur content of No. 2 fuel oil burned in the city is _____%.

    A. 0.1 B. 0.2 C. 0.3 D. 0.4

13. A 35% volatile matter coal is

    A. lignite
    B. semi-bituminous
    C. bituminous
    D. anthracite

14. Which coal will give off the MOST smoke?

    A. Graphite
    B. Anthracite
    C. Bituminous
    D. Lignite

15. *Pocahontas* is a type of coal which is

    A. semi-bituminous
    B. mined in Northern Pennsylvania and has 15.390 BTU
    C. a low grade anthracite
    D. mined in Virginia and is of good quality

16. Bituminous coal is NOT a _____ volatile coal.

    A. low B. medium C. high D. 5%

17. The volatile matter in bituminous coal ranges from

    A. 2 to 5% B. 5 to 20% C. 20 to 40% D. 40 to 60%

18. The percentage of volatile combustible matter in a soft coal from the west Pennsylvania high volatile field would be MOST NEARLY _____%.

    A. 10 B. 30 C. 50 D. 70

19. Plants operating in the city would MOST likely be burning coal with a moisture content of _____%.

    A. 25 B. 15 C. 10 D. 5

20. In referring to fusion temperature, we are USUALLY speaking of

    A. ash B. coke C. coal D. oil

21. Clinkering in a furnace is due MAINLY to too

    A. high a percentage of ash in the fuel
    B. low a fusion temperature of ash
    C. high a fusion temperature of ash
    D. low a percentage of ash in the coal

22. The slagging and clinkering properties of coals can be determined by

    A. proximate analysis
    B. ultimate analysis
    C. ash fusion temperature
    D. percent of ash

23. The *burning* characteristic of coal MOST closely related to ash fusion temperatures is

    A. coking
    B. caking
    C. clinkering
    D. free burning

24. In comparison to anthracite or bituminous coal, an equal weight of coke would

    A. take up a greater volume in bin
    B. take up a lesser volume in bin
    C. require more air for combustion
    D. none of the above

25. Which type of coal is MOST likely to slack (turn to dust) when left lying around in open air?

    A. Anthracite
    B. Bituminous
    C. Sub-bituminous
    D. Lignite

KEY(CORRECT ANSWERS)

1. A		11. D	
2. D		12. B	
3. B		13. A	
4. C		14. C	
5. A		15. A	
6. B		16. C	
7. B		17. C	
8. C		18. B	
9. C		19. D	
10. B		20. A	

21. B
22. C
23. A
24. A
25. D

TEST 2

DIRECTIONS: Each question or incomplete statement is followed by several suggested answers or completions. Select the one that BEST answers the question or completes the Statement. *PRINT THE LETTER OF THE CORRECT ANSWER IN THE SPACE AT THE RIGHT.*

1. The one of the following that lists the size classifications of anthracite coal in PROPER order ranging from the smallest to the largest is 1.____

   A. chestnut, culm, pea, birdseye, egg
   B. egg, stove, pea, broken, culm
   C. stove, egg, birdseye, culm, broken
   D. birdseye, pea, chestnut, stove, eag

2. The fire in a hand-fired furnace can be cleaned by a method known as 2.____

   A. *ashpit to grate*   B. *bottom to top*
   C. *side to side*   D. *grate to crown*

3. Coal is normally *tempered* when operating a chain-grate stoker for the purpose of 3.____

   A. increasing coking   B. preventing clinking
   C. collecting particles   D. promoting uniform burning

4. The one of the following coals that can LEGALLY be burned in city power plants is 4.____

   A. anthracite   B. sub-bituminous
   C. non-coking   D. bituminous

5. The one of the following that is known as *rice coal* is _____ coal. 5.____

   A. pea   B. buckwheat No. 2
   C. egg   D. culm

6. The instrument used to measure atmospheric pressure is a 6.____

   A. capillary tube   B. venturi
   C. barometer   D. calorimeter

7. The control which starts or stops the operation of the oil burner at a predetermined steam pressure is the 7.____

   A. pressuretrol   B. air flow interlock
   C. transformer   D. magnetic oil valve

8. In a closed feedwater heater, the water and the steam 8.____

   A. come into direct contact
   B. are kept apart from each other
   C. are under negative pressure
   D. mix and exhaust into the atmosphere

9. A *knocking* noise in steam lines is GENERALLY the result of 9.____

   A. superheated steam expansion
   B. high steam pressure

C. condensation in the line
D. rapid steam expansion

10. An electrical component known as a step-up transformer operates by raising _____ and decreasing _____.

   A. voltage; amperage
   B. resistance; amperage
   C. amperage; resistance
   D. voltage and amperage; nothing

11. A manometer is an instrument that is used to measure

   A. heat radiation
   B. air volume
   C. condensate water level
   D. air pressure

12. Three 75-gallon per hour mechanical pressure type oil burners operating together are to burn 150,000 gallons of No. 6 fuel oil.
    The number of hours they would take to burn this amount of oil is MOST NEARLY

   A. 665   B. 760   C. 870   D. 1210

13. A MAJOR cause of air pollution resulting from the burning of fuel oils is _____ dioxide.

   A. sulfur   B. silicon   C. nitrous   D. hydrogen

14. The CO_2 percentage in the flue gas of a power plant is indicated by a

   A. Doppler meter
   B. Ranarex indicator
   C. microtector
   D. orsat device

15. The MOST likely cause of black smoke exhausting from the chimney of an oil-fired boiler is

   A. high secondary air flow
   B. low stack emission
   C. low oil temperature
   D. high chimney draft

16. The diameter of the steam piston in a steam-driven duplex vacuum pump whose dimensions are given as 3 by 2 by 4 is

   A. 2   B. 3   C. 4   D. 6

17. An induced draft fan is GENERALLY connected between the

   A. condenser and the first pass
   B. stack and the breeching
   C. feedwater heater and the boiler feed pump
   D. combustion chamber and fuel oil tanks

18. The purpose of an air chamber on a reciprocating water pump is to

   A. maintain a uniform flow
   B. reduce the amount of steam expansion
   C. create a pulsating flow
   D. vary the amount of steam admission

19. *Flash point* is the temperature at which oil will

   A. change completely to vapor
   B. safely fire in a furnace
   C. flash into flame if a lighted match is passed just above the top of the oil
   D. burn intermittently when ignited

20. When soot blowing water tube boilers, you blow

   A. any time
   B. with boiler in low rating
   C. after banking fires
   D. with boiler at half to full load

Questions 21-25.

DIRECTIONS: Questions 21 through 25 are to be answered on the basis of the following Information.

Fuel is conserved when a boiler is operating near its most efficient load. The efficiency of a boiler will change as the output varies. Large amounts of air must be used at low ratings, and so the heat exchange is inefficient. As the output increases, the efficiency decreases due to an increase in flue gas temperature. Every boiler has an output rate for which its efficiency is highest. For example, in a water-tube boiler, the highest efficiency might occur at 120 percent of rated capacity, while in a vertical fire-tube boiler, highest efficiency might be at 70% of rated capacity. The type of fuel burned and cleanliness affect the maximum efficiency of the boiler. When a power plant contains a battery of boilers, a sufficient number should be kept in operation so as to maintain the output of individual units near their points of maximum efficiency. One of the boilers in the battery can be used as a regulator to meet the change in demand for steam while the other boilers could still operate at their most efficient ratings. Boiler performance is expressed as the number of pounds of steam generated per pound of fuel.

21. The number of pounds of steam generated per pound of fuel is a measure of boiler

   A. size   B. performance
   C. regulator input   D. by-pass

22. The HIGHEST efficiency of a vertical fire-tube boiler might occur at _____% of _____ capacity.

   A. 70; rated   B. 80; water tube
   C. 95; water tube   D. 120; rated

23. The MAXIMUM efficiency of a boiler Is affected by

   A. atmospheric temperature   B. atmospheric pressure
   C. fire brick material   D. cleanliness

24. A heat exchanger uses large amounts of air at low

   A. fuel rates   B. ratings
   C. temperatures   D. pressure

25. One boiler in a battery of boilers should be used as a   25.____
    A. demand   B. stand-by   C. regulator   D. safety

KEY(CORRECT ANSWERS)

1. D
2. C
3. D
4. A
5. B

6. C
7. A
8. B
9. C
10. A

11. D
12. A
13. A
14. B
15. C

16. A
17. B
18. A
19. C
20. C

21. B
22. A
23. D
24. B
25. C

EXAMINATION SECTION
TEST 1

DIRECTIONS: Each question or incomplete statement is followed by several suggested answers or completions. Select the one that BEST answers the question or completes the statement. *PRINT THE LETTER OF THE CORRECT ANSWER IN THE SPACE AT THE RIGHT.*

1. The slope characteristic necessary to classify a soil quantity as having only slight limitations for development as an area landfill site is _____ %. 1._____
   A. 0 B. 0-8 C. 0-15 D. over 8

2. On average, the amount of municipal refuse produced by a single person in one day is APPROXIMATELY _____ pounds. 2._____
   A. 1.5-2.5 B. 2.0-3.5 C. 3.5-5.5 D. 4-6.5

3. The percentage of solid waste in the United States direct-ly disposed of on land is APPROXIMATELY _____ %. 3._____
   A. 40 B. 55 C. 70 D. 85

4. What device is used for the monitoring and study of land-fill leachate? 4._____
   A. Precipitator
   B. Deglasser
   C. Lysimeter
   D. Manometer

5. Which stage in the approval of a landfill site would occur LAST? 5._____
   A. Hearing
   B. Appeals
   C. Site selection
   D. Study

6. Site development plans for a sanitary landfill should include initial and final topography at a contour interval of _____ meter(s) or _____ . 6._____
   A. 1; more
   B. 1.5; less
   C. 2; more
   D. 2.5; less

7. Which piece of landfill equipment or machinery is MOST effective for spreading solid waste? 7._____
   A. Crawler loader
   B. Dragline
   C. Rubber-tired loader
   D. Crawler dozer

8. The cover material BEST suited for keeping burrowing animals from penetrating a landfill site is 8._____
   A. clay
   B. gravel
   C. clean sand
   D. silty sand

9. The recommended number of equipment operators for use at a landfill site handling 500 tons of waste per day is 9._____
   A. 1 B. 2 C. 6 D. 12

10. What accounts for the GREATEST portion of a sanitary landfill's operating costs?

    A. Administration B. Equipment
    C. Overhead D. Wages

11. In a typical sanitary landfill leachate quantity, _____ is found to be in the HIGHEST concentration.

    A. chloride B. lead C. sodium D. zinc

12. Under normal conditions, miles is considered to be economical for collection vehicles that deliver solid waste to a landfill site.

    A. 5-15 B. 15-30 C. 25-40 D. 30-50

13. In order to be classified as *high density,* baled solid waste must be baled to _____ pounds per cubic foot.

    A. 40-60 B. 50-60 C. 60-70 D. 75-90

14. Clay liners are used in many landfill sites to prevent or *attenuate* the seepage of chemicals and organic material. For which of the following substances would a clay liner be rated as having *moderate* attenuation qualities?

    A. Mercury B. Lead C. Iron D. Calcium

15. Groundwater monitoring systems used at a landfill site typically include AT LEAST _____ monitoring well(s) down-gradient from the site.

    A. 1 B. 1-2 C. 2-3 D. 2-5

16. The LEAST effective method for the treatment of strong landfill leachates is

    A. rotating biological contractors
    B. anaerobic digesters
    C. trickling filters
    D. aerated lagoons

17. The MOST effective device for monitoring and analyzing landfill gases is a

    A. lysimeter B. dry well
    C. steel probe D. gas chromatograph

18. In order to classify a soil quantity as having only slight limitations for development as a trench landfill site, _____ inches of soil above hard bedrock is necessary.

    A. 36-48 B. 48-60
    C. 60-72 D. more than 72

19. The common landfill practice for disposal of bulky wastes such as car bodies is to

    A. dig a hole in the working face in order to backfill the heavier wastes
    B. place them on the surface of the working face, at the bottom
    C. place them on the surface of the working face, in the middle
    D. spread them evenly over the top of the landfill site, just before applying cover material

20. Which ionic substance is MOST commonly used as a tracer for tracking landfill leachate influence on an area's groundwater supply? 20.____

    A. Nitrogen   B. Chloride   C. Sodium   D. Sulfide

21. Under normal conditions, baled waste can be expected to *rebound,* or re-expand, to an extent of _____ %. 21.____

    A. 5-10   B. 10-15   C. 20-30   D. 35-50

22. Under normal conditions, _____ cubic yards of landfill space are needed to meet the annual needs of a municipal population of approximately 10,000. 22.____

    A. 4,000-16,000
    B. 12,000-26,000
    C. 16,000-32,000
    D. 24,000-48,000

23. Until conditions have been found to be satisfactory for two consecutive inspections at a new or probationary landfill site, federal regulations require a state or local inspection 23.____

    A. semi-monthly
    B. monthly
    C. every six months
    D. annually

24. A crawler dozer at a landfill site can be used economically for moving earth or waste over distances of up to 24.____

    A. 100 feet
    B. 300 feet
    C. one-fourth of a mile
    D. one mile

25. When spreading solid waste into layers at a landfill site, each layer should be no more than _____ feet deep. 25.____

    A. 2   B. 4   C. 6   D. 12

KEY (CORRECT ANSWERS)

1. B		11. A	
2. C		12. C	
3. D		13. C	
4. C		14. C	
5. B		15. C	
6. B		16. C	
7. D		17. D	
8. B		18. D	
9. B		19. B	
10. D		20. B	

21. B
22. C
23. B
24. B
25. A

TEST 2

DIRECTIONS: Each question or incomplete statement is followed by several suggested answers or completions. Select the one that BEST answers the question or completes the statement. *PRINT THE LETTER OF THE CORRECT ANSWER IN THE SPACE AT THE RIGHT.*

1. The MOST expensive material for use as a sanitary landfill liner is 1.____

    A. butyl rubber B. Hypalon
    C. chlorinated polyethylene D. polyvinyl chloride

2. The depth of cover material recommended for an area in which new cells will NOT be added for at least 30 days is 2.____

    A. 1 inch B. 6 inches C. 1 foot D. 2 feet

3. What is the term for the two-piece hydraulic bucket used on loaders at a landfill site? 3.____

    A. Grapple B. Bullclam
    C. Grouser D. U-blade

4. MOST rubber-tired equipment used at landfill sites can be operated economically at distances of up to 4.____

    A. 300 feet B. 600 feet
    C. half a mile D. one mile

5. The percentage of a landfill's total operating expenses consumed by the cost of monitoring operations is _____ %. 5.____

    A. 0-1 B. 2-5 C. 5-8 D. 8-12

6. The BEST possible soil type for excavating and working a trench landfill site is 6.____

    A. silty sand B. clay
    C. sandy loam D. clayey-silty sand

7. What type of landfill equipment or machinery is MOST effective for use in large excavation operations? 7.____

    A. Landfill compactor B. Dragline
    C. Rubber-tired loader D. Scraper

8. Clay landfill liners have proven virtually incapable of seepage prevention of 8.____

    A. mercury B. zinc C. potassium D. calcium

9. The typical moisture content of mixed municipal solid waste is _____ %. 9.____

    A. 3-5 B. 10-18 C. 20-30 D. 25-40

10. What permeability rate, in inches per hour, is the MINIMUM necessary in order to classify a soil quantity as having only slight limitations for development as an area landfill site? 10.____

    A. 1 B. 2 C. 3 D. 4

11. The MAXIMUM waste cell density, in pounds per cubic yard, that can be achieved through *moderate* compacting efforts is 11.____

    A. 500 B. 800 C. 1000 D. 1500

12. The MAXIMUM haul capacity, in pounds per cubic yard, for most scrapers used at a landfill site is 12._____

    A. 2 B. 12 C. 28 D. 40

13. What type of landfill equipment or machinery is MOST effective for spreading cover material over a landfill cell or site? 13._____

    A. Rubber-tired loader B. Crawler dozer
    C. Dragline D. Landfill compactor

14. The term for the vertical distance of a compacted volume of solid waste plus the thickness of the waste's cover material is called 14._____

    A. cell depth B. cell thickness
    C. trench height D. lift depth

15. When using a dragline during trench landfill operations, the guideline for the dragline's boom length is _____ the trench _____. 15._____

    A. half; depth B. twice; depth
    C. half; width D. twice; width

16. After a landfill's final cover has been graded to the desired level, stakes with _____ tops are planted on the surface to signal completion. 16._____

    A. green B. red C. orange D. blue

17. Industry standards require that no solid waste, regardless of its type, should be exposed for a period of more than 17._____

    A. 6 hours B. 12 hours C. 24 hours D. two days

18. The cover material BEST suited for the growing of vegetation over a completed landfill site is 18._____

    A. silt B. clayey-silty sand
    C. clean sand D. clay

19. Which of the following landfill vehicles is the quickest and most mobile during operation? 19._____

    A. Rubber-tired loader B. Dozer
    C. Landfill compactor D. Dragline

20. The problem of gas migration within a landfill can be solved by either active or passive methods. 20._____
    Which of the following statements about passive gas migration control is FALSE?
    It

    A. is limited to shallow sites
    B. involves the installation of venting trenches backfilled with stone
    C. uses natural vacuums to control gases
    D. is typically employed beyond the landfill boundary

21. The MINIMUM recommended density, in pounds per cubic yard (lb/yd^3), for compacted waste cells in a sanitary landfill is

    A. 500 B. 800 C. 1000 D. 1500

22. The GREATEST danger to people at or near a sanitary landfill site is from

    A. equipment failure
    B. gas production
    C. dioxin poisoning
    D. organic water pollution

23. Which organic waste's decomposition generates the GREATEST amount of gas within a landfill?

    A. Protein
    B. Cellulose
    C. Carbohydrate
    D. Fat

24. The impermeable liner that is placed below the base of a landfill site to prevent seepage is USUALLY _____ in thickness.

    A. 6-12 inches
    B. 12-28 inches
    C. 1-3 feet
    D. 2-6 feet

25. According to industry recommendations, the MINIMUM number of personnel used to operate a landfill site should be

    A. 2 B. 3 C. 4 D. 5

KEY (CORRECT ANSWERS)

1. A		11. C	
2. C		12. D	
3. B		13. B	
4. B		14. D	
5. B		15. D	
6. B		16. D	
7. B		17. B	
8. D		18. B	
9. C		19. A	
10. B		20. C	

21. B
22. B
23. D
24. C
25. A

EXAMINATION SECTION
TEST 1

DIRECTIONS: Each question or incomplete statement is followed by several suggested answers or completions. Select the one that BEST answers the question or completes the statement. *PRINT THE LETTER OF THE CORRECT ANSWER IN THE SPACE AT THE RIGHT.*

1. A self-propelled scraper used at landfill sites can haul cover material economically at distances of up to

    A. 300 feet   B. 500 feet   C. 1000 feet   D. one mile

2. The MINIMUM depth of cover material recommended for final application over a worked landfill area (one that is to remain idle for at least one year) is

    A. 1 inch   B. 6 inches   C. 1 foot   D. 2 feet

3. The type of vent preferred at landfill sites for the control of gas production is a

    A. Tiki burner   B. open riser
    C. Du Page riser   D. suction borehole

4. The typical capacity, in cubic yards, of a dragline bucket is

    A. .5-2   B. 1-3   C. 3-5   D. 8-12

5. The recommended number of weighmasters at a landfill site handling 4,000 tons of waste per day is

    A. 1   B. 3   C. 5   D. 8

6. _____ inches above the water table are necessary in order to classify a soil quantity as having only slight limitations for development as a trench landfill site.

    A. More than 60   B. 48-60
    C. 36-48   D. 24-36

7. Which of the following substances is suitable for disposal in a sanitary landfill?

    A. Aluminum fluoride   B. Lead
    C. Sodium oxide   D. Sulfur

8. Site development plans for a sanitary landfill should include the location of all utilities within _____ of the proposed site.

    A. 200 feet   B. 500 feet
    C. half a mile   D. one mile

9. The synthetic liner material MOST resistant to petroleum solvents is

    A. butyl rubber
    B. neoprene
    C. polyvinyl chloride
    D. chloro-sulfonated polyethylene

10. Typically, cold climate landfills require _____ feet of insulating material to be used on the prepared ground.

    A. 2 B. 3 C. 6 D. 9

11. Which stage in the approval of a landfill site would occur FIRST?

    A. Hearing B. Appeals
    C. Site selection D. Study

12. The method for controlling landfill gas migration potentially MOST dangerous would be using

    A. an impermeable liner and impermeable final cover material
    B. an impermeable liner and venting only on the downgrade side
    C. a permeable liner with an impermeable cover material
    D. vent burners above a permeable cover layer

13. The GREATEST influence on a landfill's rate of settlement is from

    A. compaction B. water
    C. temperature D. cover material

14. The slope characteristic necessary to classify a soil quantity as having only slight limitations for development as a trench landfill site is _____ %.

    A. 0 B. 0-8 C. 0-15 D. over 8

15. What is the term for the perpendicular distance between quantities of cover material that had been placed over the last working faces of two successive cells in a sanitary landfill?

    A. Cell depth B. Cell thickness
    C. Trench height D. Lift depth

16. Clay liners at landfill sites are typically MOST effective at preventing the seepage of

    A. chloride B. magnesium C. lead D. potassium

17. Economic conditions generally favor large-capacity landfill sites that can be used for AT LEAST _____ years.

    A. 5 B. 15 C. 25 D. 40

18. When present in a quantity of solid waste, which substance in its cationic form is MOST effective at inhibiting the generation of methane gas?

    A. Potassium B. Ammonium
    C. Sodium D. Calcium

19. All of the following are factors involved in determining the amount of space needed for municipal refuse disposal EXCEPT

    A. total amount of earth cover used
    B. per capita refuse contribution
    C. density of loose, delivered waste
    D. time span of site use

20. What type of landfill equipment or machinery is used for hauling cover material? 20.____
    A. Scraper
    B. Rubber-tired loader
    C. Crawler loader
    D. Landfill compactor

21. The industry recommendation for the top cover on a landfill site is a grade of no less than _____%. 21.____
    A. 1
    B. 2
    C. 4
    D. 6

22. The LEAST expensive material for use as a sanitary landfill liner is 22.____
    A. hot-sprayed asphalt
    B. soil cement with sealer
    C. polyethylene
    D. polyvinyl chloride

23. For short peak periods during landfill operation, an experienced weighmaster can be expected to manually record the net weight and types of material delivered to a landfill at a rate of _____ trucks per hour. 23.____
    A. 15
    B. 30
    C. 60
    D. 100

24. _____ inches above rippable bedrock are necessary in order to classify a soil quantity as having only slight limitations for development as a trench landfill site. 24.____
    A. More than 60
    B. 48-60
    C. 36-48
    D. 24-36

25. The device used to increase the traction of an off-highway crawler tractor used at a landfill site is a 25.____
    A. ripper
    B. scarifier
    C. clam
    D. grouser

KEY (CORRECT ANSWERS)

1. C		11. C	
2. D		12. A	
3. A		13. B	
4. B		14. C	
5. B		15. B	
6. A		16. C	
7. D		17. B	
8. B		18. A	
9. B		19. C	
10. B		20. A	

21. B
22. C
23. C
24. A
25. D

TEST 2

DIRECTIONS: Each question or incomplete statement is followed by several suggested answers or completions. Select the one that BEST answers the question or completes the statement. *PRINT THE LETTER OF THE CORRECT ANSWER IN THE SPACE AT THE RIGHT.*

1. Typically, more than one piece of landfill equipment will be required at sites that serve a municipal population of more than

    A. 1000   B. 10,000   C. 100,000   D. 1,000,000

    1._____

2. The two principal gases produced by the decomposition of landfill wastes are

    A. carbon dioxide and ozone
    B. methane and oxygen
    C. oxygen and hydrogen sulfide
    D. carbon dioxide and methane

    2._____

3. Given waste generation and waste density near the industry norm, _____ acre-feet would be required annually for a municipal population of 10,000.

    A. 15   B. 30   C. 85   D. 150

    3._____

4. The base of any proposed landfill should be _____ feet above the shallowest area aquifer.

    A. less than 3-7   B. less than 6-9
    C. more than 3-7   D. more than 6-9

    4._____

5. During the first few days following the cover of a landfill site or cell, the principal gas that is produced by the organic decomposition of landfill waste is

    A. oxygen   B. methane
    C. carbon dioxide   D. hydrogen sulfide

    5._____

6. In a typical sanitary landfill leachate quantity, _____ is found to be in the LOWEST concentration.

    A. magnesium   B. calcium   C. copper   D. iron

    6._____

7. After conditions have been found to be satisfactory for two consecutive inspections at a landfill site, federal regulations require a state or local inspection to take place

    A. semi-monthly   B. monthly
    C. every six months   D. annually

    7._____

8. In the development of a landfill site, the MINIMUM recommended distance from streams, lakes, and other bodies of water is

    A. 200 feet   B. 500 feet
    C. half a mile   D. one mile

    8._____

9. Industry estimates indicate that the amount of municipal refuse increases at an APPROXIMATE rate of _____ % annually.

    A. .5   B. 4   C. 12   D. 20

    9._____

10. The recommended number of equipment operators at a landfill site handling 4000 tons of waste per day is 10.____

    A. 4 B. 6 C. 8 D. 12

11. The cover material BEST suited for preventing the emergence of flies at a landfill site is 11.____

    A. clay
    C. clayey gravel
    B. gravel
    D. clean sand

12. According to industry recommendations, collection vehicle access roadways leading to a sanitary landfill gatehouse should NOT be graded to more than _____%. 12.____

    A. 2 B. 4 C. 6 D. 8

13. The synthetic liner material MOST resistant to aromatic hydrocarbons is 13.____

    A. butyl rubber
    C. polyvinyl chloride
    B. chlorinated polyethylene
    D. polyethylene

14. What is the term for the vertical thickness of a compacted volume of solid waste that is enclosed by natural soil and/or cover material? 14.____

    A. Cell depth
    C. Trench height
    B. Cell thickness
    D. Lift depth

15. The MOST commonly reported operating problem associated with sanitary landfill sites is 15.____

    A. noise
    C. traffic problems
    B. blowing paper
    D. gas emissions

16. What depth of cover material, regardless of weather conditions, is the daily recommendation for application over a worked landfill cell or site? 16.____

    A. 1 inch B. 6 inches C. 1 foot D. 2 feet

17. The MAIN problem associated with converting a landfill's passive gas migration control system into an active system is 17.____

    A. that the gas collection pipework must be dismantled
    B. that the system will be limited to very low vacuum pressure
    C. an increase in leachate risk
    D. the costly and time-consuming backfill of venting trenches

18. What type of landfill equipment or machinery is MOST effective for excavating solid waste? 18.____

    A. Crawler loader
    C. Rubber-tired dozer
    B. Rubber-tired loader
    D. Landfill compactor

19. The distance of separation between solid waste and ground-water necessary in order to make liquid leachates bacteriologically safe is GENERALLY _____ feet. 19.____

    A. 2 B. 5 C. 8 D. 10

20. Site development plans for a sanitary landfill should include other municipal land use or zoning within _____ of the proposed site.

    A. 300 feet
    B. 800 feet
    C. a quarter of a mile
    D. one mile

21. Which of the following materials is unsuitable for disposal at a sanitary landfill site?

    A. Aluminum oxide
    B. Copper acetylide
    C. Tantalum
    D. Calcium phosphate

22. A clay liner would be rated as having *low* attenuation qualities for

    A. cadmium   B. chloride   C. mercury   D. potassium

23. What type of landfill equipment or machinery is MOST effective for use in wetland operations?

    A. Crawler dozer
    B. Dragline
    C. Landfill compactor
    D. Scraper

24. An example of *primary* leaching in a landfill's original fill would be the dissolution of

    A. chloride salts
    B. organic nitrogen
    C. ferric salts
    D. organic carbon

25. Landfills as a method of waste disposal are preferable to other methods MAINLY because they

    A. are a convenient method of waste disposal as a result of modern compaction methods
    B. eliminate local objections since the refuse is covered by sand
    C. make swampy land useful and therefore are economical
    D. provide a problem-free means of disposing of refuse

KEY (CORRECT ANSWERS)

1. C
2. D
3. A
4. D
5. C

6. C
7. C
8. A
9. B
10. D

11. A
12. D
13. D
14. A
15. B

16. B
17. B
18. A
19. B
20. C

21. B
22. B
23. B
24. A
25. C

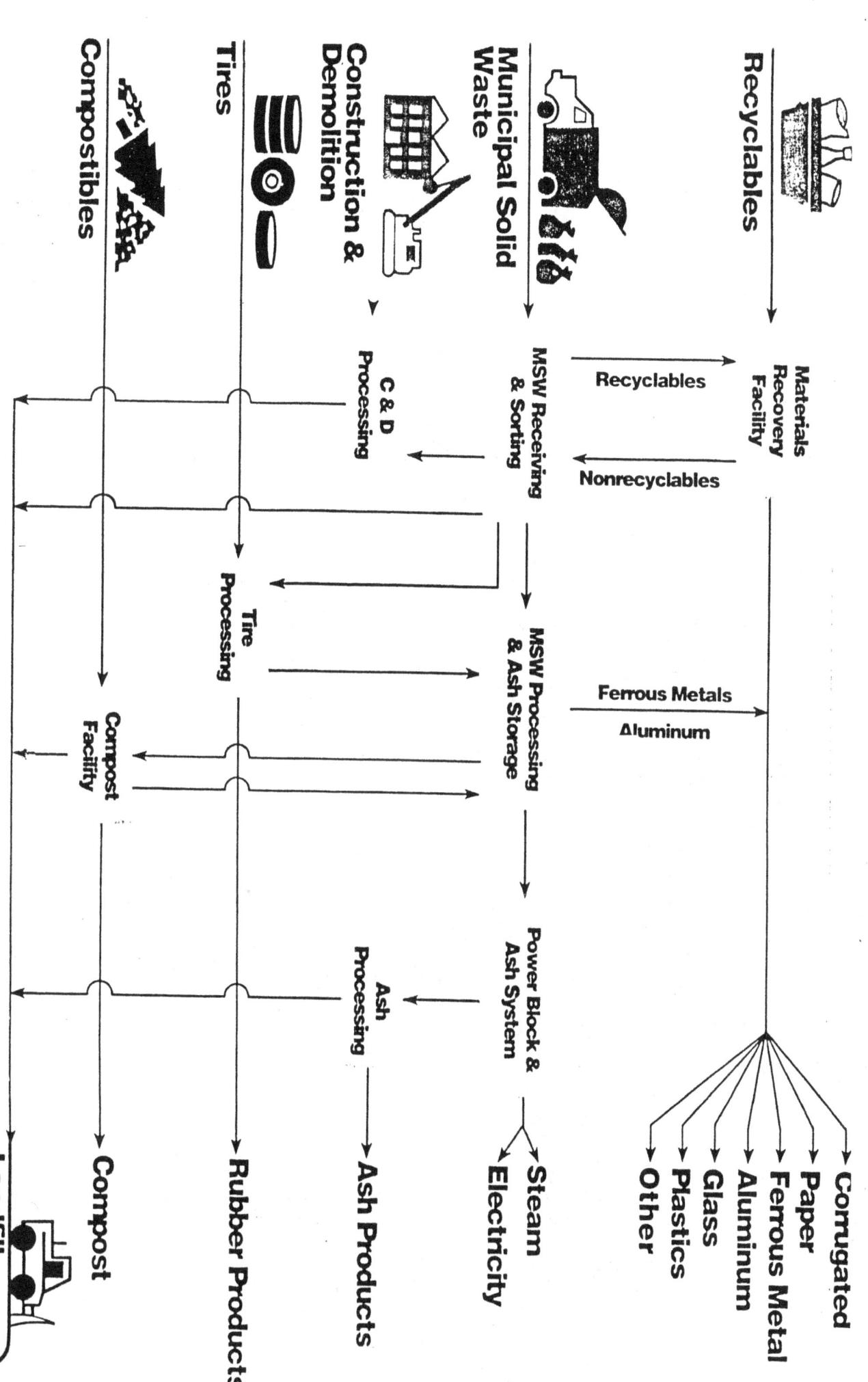

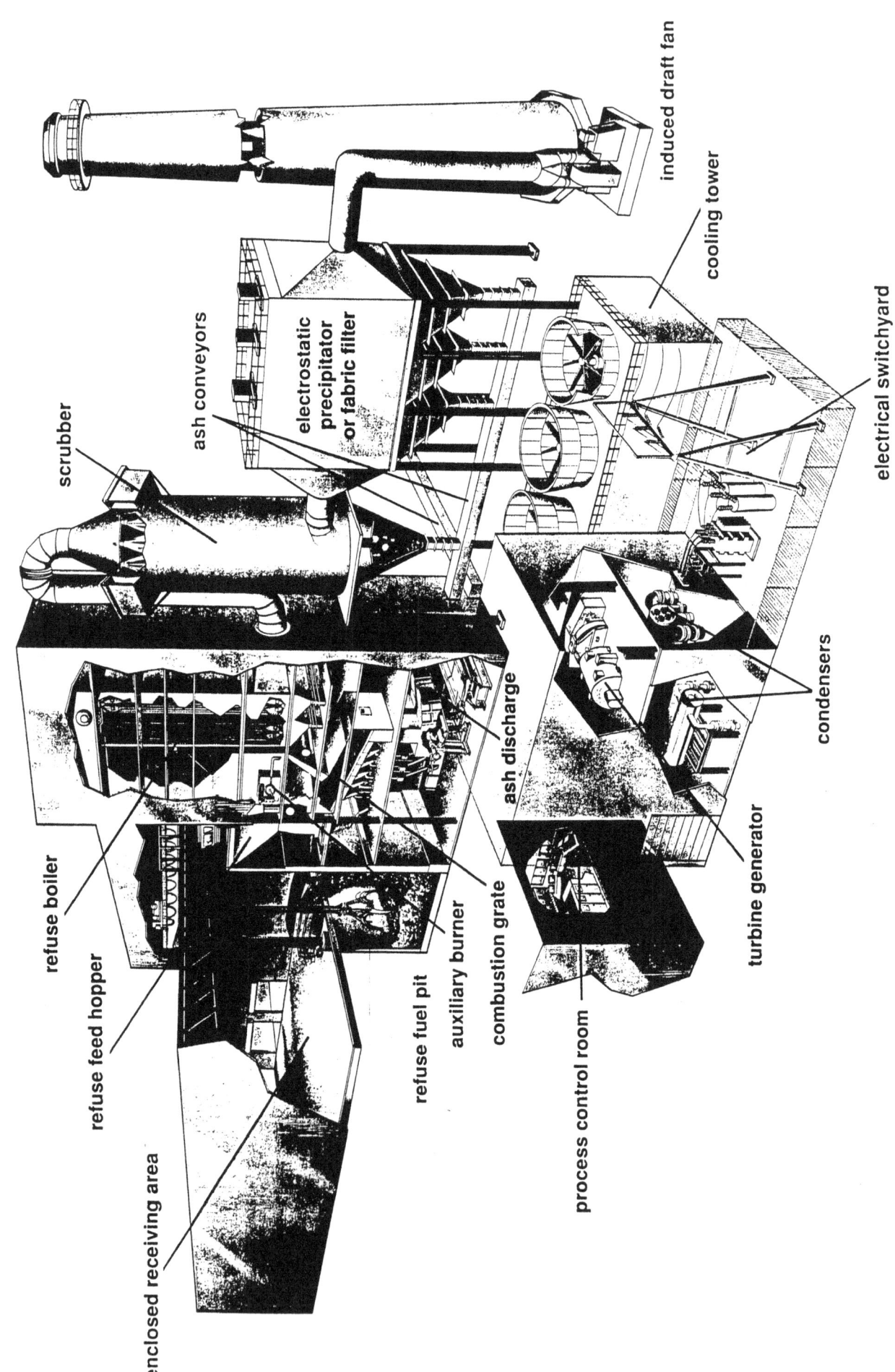